PRENTICE HALL MATHEMATICS

ALGEBRA 2

Practice Workbook

PEARSON

Prentice Hall

Needham, Massachusetts
Upper Saddle River, New Jersey
Glenview, Illinois

ISBN: 0-13-063395-X

1 2 3 4 5 6 7 8 9 10   06 05 04 03 02

PEARSON
Prentice
Hall

Practice Workbook

Contents

Answers appear in the back of each Chapter Support File.

Contents (cont.)

Practice 1-1

Properties of Real Numbers

Simplify.

1. $-|4.2|$

2. $|12 - 16|$

3. $\left|-\dfrac{7}{6}\right|$

4. $|3| - |-2|$

5. $\left|\dfrac{2}{3}\right|$

6. $0.3|-6|$

7. $|14 - 8|$

8. $|-0.01|$

Replace each $ with the symbol $<$, $>$, or $=$ to make the sentence true.

9. $-\sqrt{6}$ \$ $\sqrt{10}$

10. $\dfrac{3}{2}$ \$ 1.5

11. 0.06 \$ 0.6

12. 4 \$ $|-4|$

13. -0.4 \$ 0

14. $-|-7|$ \$ $|-7|$

15. 0.9 \$ $\dfrac{2}{3}$

16. $\sqrt{2}$ \$ $\sqrt{5}$

Name all the sets of numbers to which each number belongs.

17. -5

18. 0

19. $\sqrt{5}$

20. $2.\overline{7}$

21. 9

22. $\dfrac{10}{7}$

23. $1.2345267831\ldots$

24. $-\dfrac{4}{2}$

Name the property of real numbers illustrated by each equation.

25. $\pi + 3 = 3 + \pi$

26. $\sqrt{2} + 0 = \sqrt{2}$

27. $(2 + x) + 3 = 2 + (x + 3)$

28. $\dfrac{5}{9} \cdot \dfrac{9}{5} = 1$

29. $16(3t + 4v) = 48t + 64v$

30. $\sqrt{2} \cdot 3 = 3 \cdot \sqrt{2}$

31. $0.01 \cdot 1 = 0.01$

32. $\dfrac{3}{2} \cdot \dfrac{2}{3} = 1$

33. $7 + (-7) = 0$

34. $2(xy) = (2x)y$

Graph the number on the following number line. Estimate if necessary.

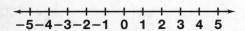

35. $-\sqrt{2}$

36. $\dfrac{3}{2}$

37. 0.5

38. -1

Find the opposite and the reciprocal of each number.

39. $-2\dfrac{1}{2}$

40. 3

41. $\dfrac{5}{9}$

42. -4

Which set of numbers best describes the values of each variable?

43. the number of stops N a commuter train makes on a certain day

44. the high H and low L for a certain stock during a period of n weeks

45. the average time per lap t it takes a race car to complete n laps

Practice 1-2 **Algebraic Expressions**

• •

Simplify by combining like terms.

1. $6x + x$

2. $11t + 3t - 5$

3. $-6a - 5a + b - 1$

4. $5i + 7j - 3i$

5. $16xy - 4xy$

6. $5x - 3x^2 + 16x^2$

7. $3(m - 2) + m$

8. $\dfrac{3(a - b)}{9} + \dfrac{4}{9}b$

9. $t + \dfrac{t^2}{2} + t^2 + t$

10. $4a - 5(a + 1)$

11. $2(m - n^2) - 6(n^2 + 3m)$

12. $x(x - y) + y(y - x)$

13. The expression $6s^2$ represents the surface area of a cube with edges of length s. Find the surface area of a cube with each edge length.

    a. 3 inches   **b.** 1.5 meters

14. The expression $4.95 + 0.07x$ models a household's monthly long-distance charges, where x represents the number of minutes of long-distance calls during the month. Find the monthly charges for 73 minutes.

Evaluate each expression for the given value of the variable.

15. $5y^2 + y + 1;\, y = 4$

16. $a + 6 + 3a;\, a = 5$

17. $-t^2 - (3t + 2);\, t = 5$

18. $i^2 - 5(i^3 - i^2);\, i = 7$

19. $k + 2 - 4k - 1;\, k = -3$

20. $6a - 3a^2 - 2a^3;\, a = 1$

21. $-m(2m + m^2);\, m = -4$

22. $3 - 2n - 5 + n^2;\, n = -3$

23. $12b - 3 + b^2;\, b = 9$

24. $a^2 + b^2;\, a = 3, b = 4$

25. $c(3 - a) - c^2;\, a = 4, c = -1$

26. $-a^2 + 3(d - 2a);\, a = 2, d = -3$

27. Write an expression for the perimeter of the figure as the sum of the lengths of its sides. Then simplify your answer.

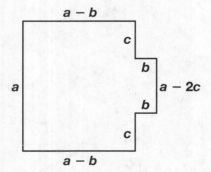

Practice 1-3

Solving Equations

Solve each formula for the indicated variable.

1. $V = \frac{\pi}{3} r^2 h$, for h

2. $S = L(1 - r)$, for r

3. $S = \ell w + wh + \ell h$, for w

Solve for *x*. State any restrictions on the variables.

4. $\frac{4}{9}(x + 3) = g$

5. $a(x + c) = b(x - c)$

6. $\frac{x + 3}{t} = t^2$

7. Two brothers are saving money to buy tickets to a concert. Their combined savings is \$55. One brother has \$15 more than the other. How much has each saved?

8. The sides of a triangle are in the ratio 5 : 12 : 13. What is the length of each side of the triangle if the perimeter of the triangle is 15 in.?

9. Find three consecutive numbers whose sum is 126.

Solve each equation.

10. $\frac{1}{2}(x - 3) + \left(\frac{3}{2} - x\right) = 5x$

11. $5w + 8 - 12w = 16 - 15w$

12. $7y + 5 = 6y + 11$

13. $1.2(x + 5) = 1.6(2x + 5)$

14. $t - 3\left(t + \frac{4}{3}\right) = 2t + 3$

15. $0.5(c + 2.8) - c = 0.6c + 0.3$

16. $3(x + 1) = 2(x + 11)$

17. $\frac{u}{5} + \frac{u}{10} - \frac{u}{6} = 1$

18. Mike and Adam left a bus terminal at the same time and traveled in opposite directions. Mike's bus was in heavy traffic and had to travel 20 mi/h slower than Adam's bus. After 3 hours, their buses were 270 miles apart. How fast was each bus going?

19. Two trains left a station at the same time. One traveled north at a certain speed and the other traveled south at twice the speed. After 4 hours, the trains were 600 miles apart. How fast was each train traveling?

20. Find four consecutive odd integers whose sum is 336.

21. The length of a rectangle is 5 cm greater than its width. The perimeter is 58 cm. Find the dimensions of the rectangle.

Practice 1-4

Solve each inequality. Graph the solutions.

1. $16 - 4t \leq 36$

2. $2(m + 3) + 1 > 23$

3. $7 + 13(x + 1) \leq 3x$

4. $-6a < 21$

5. $\frac{2}{3}(4x + 5) > \frac{9}{4}x$

6. $2[5x - (3x - 4)] < 3(2x + 3)$

7. $8(x - 5) \geq 56$

8. $6 - x \leq 7x + 3$

9. $10 - x \geq -2(3 + x)$

Solve each compound inequality. Graph the solutions.

10. $-9 \leq 4x + 3 \leq 11$

11. $16x \leq 32$ or $-5x < -40$

12. $9x < 54$ and $-4x < 12$

13. $6(x + 2) \geq 24$ or $5x + 10 \leq 15$

14. $14 > 3x - 1 \geq -10$

15. $4 < 1 - 3x < 7$

16. $2(x - 1) < -4$ or $2(x - 1) > 4$

17. $3x - 5 \geq -8$ and $3x - 5 \leq 1$

Solve each problem by writing an inequality.

18. A salesperson earns $350 per week plus 10% of her weekly sales. Find the sales necessary for the salesperson to earn at least $800 in one week.

19. The length of a rectangular yard is 50 ft, and its perimeter is less than 170 ft. Describe the width of the yard.

20. Xul is two years older than his sister Maria. The sum of their ages is greater than 32. Describe Maria's age.

21. A research team estimates that 30% of their questionnaires will not be returned. How many questionnaires should they mail out in order to be reasonably certain that at least 750 will be returned?

Solve each problem by writing a compound inequality.

22. Watermelons cost $.39 per pound at a local market. Kent's watermelon cost between $4.00 and $5.00. What are the possible weights of his watermelon?

23. How much must a carpenter cut off a 48-inch board if the length must be 40 ± 0.25 inches?

24. A concrete slab requires between 10 and 12 yd^3 of concrete. If 2.5 yd^3 of concrete can be poured each hour, how long will it take to pour the slab?

Practice 1-5

Absolute Value Equations and Inequalities

Write each specification as an absolute value inequality.

1. $6.3 \leq h \leq 10.3$ **2.** $-2.5 \leq a \leq 2.5$ **3.** $22 \leq x \leq 33$

Solve each inequality. Graph the solutions.

4. $|x + 5| > 12$ **5.** $|k - 3| \leq 19$ **6.** $|x + 2| \geq 0$

7. $2|t - 5| < 14$ **8.** $|3x - 2| + 7 \geq 11$ **9.** $5|2b + 1| - 3 \leq 7$

10. $|2 - 3w| \geq 4$ **11.** $-3|7m - 8| < 5$ **12.** $|2u| > 6$

Solve each equation. Check for extraneous solutions.

13. $|4x| = 28$ **14.** $|3x + 6| = -12$ **15.** $|z - 1| = 7z - 13$

16. $|s + 12| = 15$ **17.** $|-3x| = 63$ **18.** $2|5x + 3| = 16$

19. $|6x + 7| = 5x + 2$ **20.** $|7r - 4| = 24$ **21.** $|3c| + 2 = 11$

22. $5|x + 1| + 6 = 21$ **23.** $|3x + 5| - 2x = 3x + 4$ **24.** $-|d + 2| = 7$

Write an absolute value inequality and a compound inequality for each length x with the given tolerance.

25. a length of 4.2 cm with a tolerance of 0.01 cm

26. a length of 3.5 m with a tolerance of 0.2 cm

27. a length of 10 ft with a tolerance of 1 in.

28. Write an absolute value inequality and a compound inequality for the temperature T that was recorded to be as low as 65°F and as high as 87°F on a certain day.

29. The weight of a 40-lb bag of fertilizer varies as much as 4 oz from the stated weight. Write an absolute value inequality and a compound inequality for the weight w of a bag of fertilizer.

30. The duration of a telephone call to a software company's help desk is at least 2.5 minutes and at most 25 minutes. Write an absolute value inequality and a compound inequality for the duration d of a telephone call.

Practice 1-6

Probability

1. You select a number at random from the sample space {1, 2, 3, 4, 5}. Find each theoretical probability.

   a. P(the number is 2)

   b. P(the number is even)

   c. P(the number is prime)

   d. P(the number is less than 5)

2. In a class of 19 students, 10 study Spanish, 7 study French, and 2 study both French and Spanish. One student is picked at random. Find each probability.

   a. P(studying Spanish but not French)

   b. P(studying neither Spanish nor French)

   c. P(studying both Spanish and French)

   d. P(studying French)

3. In a telephone survey of 150 households, 75 respondents answered "Yes" to a particular question, 50 answered "No," and 25 were "Not sure." Find each experimental probability.

   a. P(answer was "Yes")

   b. P(answer was "No")

   c. P(answer was "Not sure")

   d. P(answer was not "Not sure")

4. A wallet contains four bills with denominations of $1, $5, $10, and $20. You choose two of the four bills from the wallet at random and add the dollar amounts.

   a. What is the sample space? How many outcomes are there?

   b. What is the probability of getting $15?

   c. What is the probability of getting $50?

   d. What is the probability of getting at least $25?

5. A basketball player has attempted 24 shots and made 13. Find the experimental probability that the player will make the next shot that she attempts.

6. A baseball player attempted to steal a base 70 times and was successful 47 times. Find the experimental probability that the player will be successful on his next attempt to steal a base.

For Exercises 7–8, define a simulation by telling how you represent correct answers, incorrect answers, and the quiz. Use your simulation to find each experimental probability.

7. If you guess the answers at random, what is the probability of getting at least three correct answers on a four-question true-false quiz?

8. A five-question multiple-choice quiz has four choices for each answer. If you guess the answers at random, what is the probability of getting at least four correct answers?

9. A circular pool of radius 12 ft is enclosed within a rectangular yard measuring 50 ft by 100 ft. If a ball from an adjacent golf course lands at a random point within the yard, what is the probability that the ball lands in the pool?

10. Five people each flip a coin. What is the theoretical probability that all five will get heads?

Practice 2-1

Relations and Functions

For each function, find $f(-2)$, $f\left(-\dfrac{1}{2}\right)$, $f(3)$, and $f(7)$.

1. $f(x) = 5x + 2$ **2.** $f(x) = -\dfrac{1}{3}x + 1$ **3.** $f(x) = -3x + 1.8$

Use the vertical line test to determine whether each graph represents a function.

4.
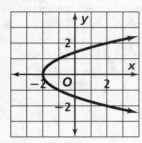

5.
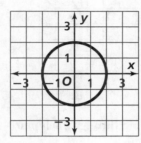

6.
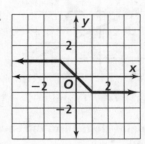

Graph each relation. Find the domain and range.

7. $\left\{(1, -2), \left(2, \dfrac{3}{4}\right), \left(3, 3\dfrac{1}{2}\right), (5, 9)\right\}$ **8.** $\{(-3, 5), (0, -2), (0, 4), (1, -2)\}$

9. $\{(-1, 2), (2, 2), (3, 2)\}$ **10.** $\{(0.5, -1), (0.5, 0). (0.5, 1), (0.5, 3)\}$

Determine whether each graph represents y as a function of x.

11.
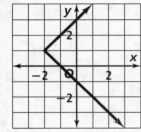

12.
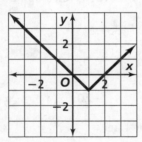

13.
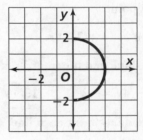

Make a mapping diagram for each relation, and determine whether it is a function.

14. $\{(1, 2), (2, 3), (2, 4), (3, 5)\}$ **15.** $\{(-1, 1), (0, 0), (1, 1), (2, 4), (3, 9)\}$

Suppose $f(x) = -3x + 2$ and $g(x) = \dfrac{1}{2}x - 1$. Find each value.

16. $f\left(\dfrac{1}{3}\right)$ **17.** $3g(4)$ **18.** $\dfrac{g(-2)}{f(3)}$ **19.** $\dfrac{f(-1)}{g(5)}$

Practice 2-2

Linear Equations

$\bullet$

Find the slope of each line.

1. $2x - 5y = 0$ **2.** $5x - y = -7$ **3.** $x - \frac{2}{3}y = \frac{1}{4}$

4. 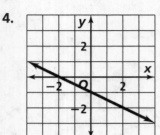   **5.** 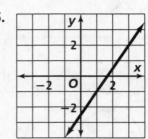   **6.**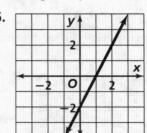

7. through $(4, -1)$ and $(-2, -3)$ **8.** through $(3, -5)$ and $(1, 2)$

Write in point-slope form the equation of the line through each pair of points.

9. $(0, 1)$ and $(3, 0)$ **10.** $\left(\frac{1}{2}, \frac{2}{3}\right)$ and $\left(-\frac{3}{2}, \frac{5}{3}\right)$ **11.** $(-3, -2)$ and $(1, 6)$

Graph each equation.

12. $4x + 3y = 12$ **13.** $\frac{x}{3} - \frac{y}{6} = 1$ **14.** $y = -\frac{3}{2}x + \frac{1}{2}$

Write in standard form an equation of the line with the given slope through the given point.

15. slope $= -4; (2, 2)$ **16.** slope $= \frac{2}{5}; (-1, 3)$ **17.** slope $= 0; (3, -4)$

Find the slope and the intercepts of each line.

18. $3x - 4y = 12$ **19.** $y = -2$ **20.** $f(x) = \frac{4}{5}x + 7$ **21.** $x = 5$

Write an equation for each line. Then graph the line.

22. through $(-1, 3)$ and parallel to $y = 2x + 1$

23. through $(2, 2)$ and perpendicular to $y = -\frac{3}{5}x + 2$

24. through $(-3, 4)$ and vertical

25. through $(4, 1)$ and horizontal

Practice 2-3

For each direct variation, find the constant of variation. Then find the value of y when $x = 3$.

1. $y = 3$ when $x = -2$

2. $y = \frac{3}{4}$ when $x = \frac{1}{8}$

3. $y = -\frac{3}{8}$ when $x = -\frac{2}{3}$

Determine whether y varies directly as x. If so, find the constant of variation.

4. $y = \frac{4}{9}x$

5. $y = -1.2x$

6. $y + 4x = 0$

7. $y - 3x = 1$

8. $y = 3x$

9. $y + 2 = x$

10. $y - \frac{3}{5}x = 0$

11. $y = -3.5x + 7$

For each function, determine whether y varies directly as x. If so, find the constant of variation and write the equation.

12.	x	y
	1	1
	2	4
	3	9

13.	x	y
	−1	−3
	1	3
	3	9

14.	x	y
	−2	−1
	2	1
	5	

15.	x	y
	−2	−3
	0	1
	1	3

Write an equation for a direct variation with a graph that passes through each point.

16. $(6, 2)$

17. $(-1.5, 9)$

18. $(-5, 90)$

19. $(7, 3)$

20. $\left(-1, -\frac{2}{3}\right)$

21. $\left(\frac{3}{5}, -\frac{7}{2}\right)$

22. $(10, 25)$

23. $(3, 165)$

In Exercises 24–27, y varies directly as x.

24. If $y = 3$ when $x = 2$, find x when $y = 5$.

25. If $y = -4$ when $x = \frac{1}{2}$, find y when $x = \frac{2}{3}$.

26. If $y = -14$ when $x = -7$, find x when $y = 22$.

27. If $y = \frac{5}{17}$ when $x = 10$, find y when $x = 5$.

28. A 15-minute long-distance telephone call costs $.90. The cost varies directly as the length of the call. Write an equation that relates the cost to the length of the call. How long is a call that costs $1.32?

29. The distance a spring stretches varies directly as the amount of weight that is hanging on it. A weight of 2.5 pounds stretches a spring 18 inches. Find the stretch of the spring when a weight of 6.4 pounds is hanging on it.

Practice 2-4

• •

Write an equation for each line.

1. y-intercept of -2.1, x-intercept of 3.5

2. through $(1.2, 5.1)$, x-intercept of 3.7

For each situation, find a linear model and use it to make a prediction.

3. The cost of producing 4 units is $204.80. The cost of producing 8 units is $209.60. How much does it cost to produce 12 units?

4. There were 174 words typed in 3 minutes. There were 348 words typed in 6 minutes. How many words will be typed in 8 minutes?

5. After 5 months the number of subscribers to a newspaper was 5730. After 7 months the number of subscribers to the newspaper was 6022. How many subscribers to the newspaper will there be after 10 months?

Graph each set of data. Decide whether a linear model is reasonable. If so, draw a trend line and write its equation.

6. $\{(1, 2.1), (3, 3.1), (5, 4.0), (7, 5.2), (9, 5.9)\}$

7. $\{(2, 3.5), (4, 4.9), (6, 6.3), (8, 4.6), (10, 2.9)\}$

8. $\{(-2, -3.9), (-1, -1.8), (0, 0.1), (1, 1.9), (2, 3.8)\}$

9. $\{(0.3, 0), (0.8, 3), (1.1, 5), (2.0, 6), (2.5, 6)\}$

10. The table shows the percentage of the population not covered by health insurance in selected states for the years 1990 and 1999.

State	Idaho	Illinois	Michigan	Montana	New York
1990	15.1	10.9	9.4	14.0	12.1
1999	19.1	14.1	11.2	18.6	16.4

Source: *The World Almanac and Book of Facts, 2001*

a. Draw a scatter plot showing the relationship between the percentage not covered by health insurance in 1990 and the percentage not covered in 1999. Use the 1990 percentage as the independent variable.

b. Use your scatter plot to develop a model relating the 1990 percentage to the 1999 percentage.

c. In Wyoming, 12.5% of the population were not covered by health insurance in 1990. Use your model to estimate the percentage who were not covered in 1999.

d. The actual percentage for Wyoming in 1999 was 16.1. Is your model reasonable?

Practice 2-5

Absolute Value Functions and Graphs

Match each equation with its graph.

1. $y = |x - 1|$

2. $y = 2|x - 1|$

3. $y = |2x| - 1$

4. $y = |x| - 1$

5. $y = |2x - 1|$

6. $y = |2x| - 2$

A.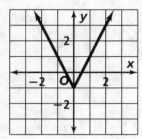

B.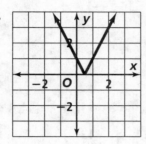

C.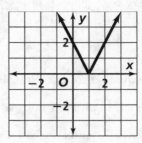

D.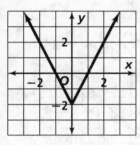

E.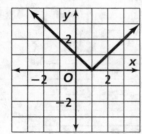

F.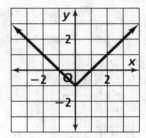

Graph each equation by writing two linear equations.

7. $y = |x - 3|$

8. $y = |2x - 5|$

9. $y = 2|x + 2|$

10. $y = |x + 3| - 1$

11. $y = -|3x + 4|$

12. $y = \left|\frac{1}{2}x - 2\right| + 1$

Graph each absolute value equation.

13. $y = |3 - x|$

14. $y = -\frac{2}{3}\left|\frac{1}{3}x\right|$

15. $y = 3 - |x + 1|$

16. $y = -|-x - 2|$

17. $3y = |2x - 9|$

18. $y = -|x| + 2$

19. $\frac{1}{2}y = |3x - 1| - 2$

20. $y + 3 = |x + 1|$

21. $-2y = |2x - 4|$

Practice 2-6

Vertical and Horizontal Translations

Describe each translation of $f(x) = |x|$ as vertical, horizontal, or diagonal. Then graph each translation.

1. $f(x) = |x + 2|$

2. $f(x) = |x + 4|$

3. $f(x) = |x| - 5$

4. $f(x) = |x + 1| - 1$

5. $f(x) = |x - 2| + 1$

6. $f(x) = \left|x - \frac{3}{2}\right|$

7. $f(x) = |x| - \frac{1}{3}$

8. $f(x) = \left|x - \frac{5}{2}\right|$

9. $f(x) = \left|x + \frac{1}{2}\right| + \frac{3}{2}$

Write an equation for each translation.

10. $y = |x|$, 1 unit up, 2 units left

11. $y = |x|$, 4 units right

12. $y = -|x|$, 3 units up, 1 unit right

13. $y = -|x|$, $\frac{3}{2}$ units down, $\frac{1}{2}$ unit right

14. $y = |x|$, 2 units down, 3 units left

15. $y = -|x|$, $\frac{3}{5}$ unit up

Write the equation of each translation of $y = x$ or $y = |x|$.

16.
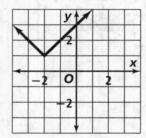

17.
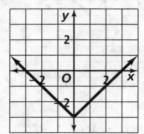

18.
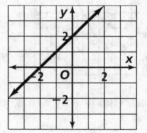

Each graph shows a translation of $y = -|x|$. State the values of h and k.

19.
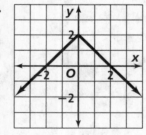

20.
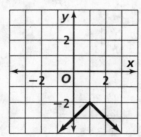

21.
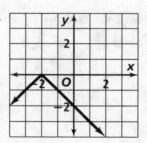

Graph each equation.

22. $y = |x - 1| + 2$

23. $y = -\left|x + \frac{1}{2}\right|$

24. $y = -|x + 3| - 1$

25. $y = |-x - 1|$

26. $y = -|x - 2| + 4$

27. $y = |x + 2| - 1$

Practice 2-7

Write an inequality for each graph. In each case, the equation for the boundary line is given.

1. $y = x - 2$

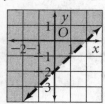

2. $x - 2y = 4$

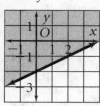

3. $y - 2x = 4$

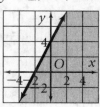

4. $y = -2$

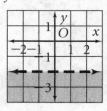

5. $x = 2$

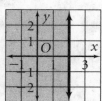

6. $-2x - 3y = 6$

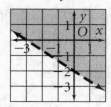

7. $3x - y = 3$

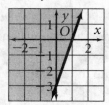

8. $y - 3x = 3$

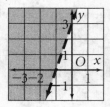

Graph each inequality on a coordinate plane.

9. $y < x$

10. $y \geq x$

11. $y > 2$

12. $y < 2$

13. $x \leq 2$

14. $x > 2$

15. $y \geq |x|$

16. $y > -2x + 1$

17. $y \geq 3x - 4$

18. $4x + 2y \leq 8$

19. $4x - 2y \leq 4$

20. $4y - 2x \geq 4$

21. $y > |x + 2|$

22. $y \leq |x - 2|$

23. $y > |x| + 2$

24. $y < |x| - 2$

25. $y \leq |4x| + 1$

26. $y \geq \left|\frac{1}{6}x\right| - 3$

27. $y > -\frac{1}{6}x - 1$

28. $3x \leq 5y$

29. You need to make at least 150 sandwiches for a picnic. You are making tuna sandwiches and ham sandwiches.

  a. Write an inequality for the number of sandwiches you can make.

  b. Graph the inequality.

  c. Does the point (90, 80) satisfy the inequality? Explain.

30. A salesperson sells two models of vacuum cleaners. One brand sells for $150 each, and the other sells for $200 each. The salesperson has a weekly sales goal of at least $1800.

  a. Write an inequality relating the revenue from the vacuum cleaners to the sales goal.

  b. Graph the inequality.

  c. If the salesperson sold exactly six $200 models last week, how many $150 models did she have to sell to make her sales goal?

Practice 3-1

Classify each system without graphing.

1. $\begin{cases} x + y = 3 \\ y = 2x - 3 \end{cases}$

2. $\begin{cases} 2x + y = 3 \\ y = -2x - 1 \end{cases}$

3. $\begin{cases} x + 3y = 9 \\ -2x - 6y = -18 \end{cases}$

4. $\begin{cases} x + y = 4 \\ y = 2x + 1 \end{cases}$

5. $\begin{cases} x + 3y = 9 \\ 9y + 3x = 27 \end{cases}$

6. $\begin{cases} x + 2y = 5 \\ 2x + 3y = 9 \end{cases}$

7. $\begin{cases} 3x + 2y = 7 \\ 3x - 15 = -6y \end{cases}$

8. $\begin{cases} x + y = 6 \\ 3x + 3y = 3 \end{cases}$

9. $\begin{cases} x + y = 11 \\ y = x - 5 \end{cases}$

10. $\begin{cases} x + 2y = 13 \\ 2y = 7 - x \end{cases}$

11. $\begin{cases} y = 12 - 5x \\ x - 4y = -6 \end{cases}$

12. $\begin{cases} 25x - 10y = 0 \\ 2y = 5x \end{cases}$

13. The spreadsheet below shows the monthly income and expenses for a new business.

   a. Find a linear model for monthly income and a linear model for monthly expenses.

   b. Use the models to estimate the month in which income will equal expenses.

	A	B	C
1	**Month**	**Income**	**Expenses**
2	May	$2000	$22,000
3	June	$3000	$18,000
4	July	$5000	$16,000
5	August	$8000	$14,000

Solve each system by graphing. Check your answers.

14. $\begin{cases} y = x - 2 \\ x + y = 10 \end{cases}$

15. $\begin{cases} y = 7 - x \\ x + 3y = 11 \end{cases}$

16. $\begin{cases} x - 2y = 10 \\ y = x - 11 \end{cases}$

17. $\begin{cases} 5x + y = 11 \\ x - y = 1 \end{cases}$

18. $\begin{cases} x + y = -1 \\ x - y = 3 \end{cases}$

19. $\begin{cases} x - y = -1 \\ 2x + 2y = 10 \end{cases}$

20. $\begin{cases} 4x + 3y = -16 \\ -x + y = 4 \end{cases}$

21. $\begin{cases} y = -3x \\ x + y = 2 \end{cases}$

22. $\begin{cases} y = \frac{2}{3}x - 5 \\ y = -\frac{2}{3}x - 3 \end{cases}$

23. $\begin{cases} y = \frac{1}{2}x + 3 \\ y = -\frac{1}{4}x - 3 \end{cases}$

24. $\begin{cases} 2x - 4y = -4 \\ 3x - y = 4 \end{cases}$

25. $\begin{cases} x + y = 6 \\ x - y = 4 \end{cases}$

Practice 3-2

Solve each system by elimination.

1. $\begin{cases} x + y = 10 \\ x - y = 2 \end{cases}$

2. $\begin{cases} -x + 3y = -1 \\ x - 2y = 2 \end{cases}$

3. $\begin{cases} x + y = 7 \\ x + 3y = 11 \end{cases}$

4. $\begin{cases} 4x - 3y = -2 \\ 4x + 5y = 14 \end{cases}$

5. $\begin{cases} x + 2y = 10 \\ 3x - y = 9 \end{cases}$

6. $\begin{cases} 2x - 5y = 11 \\ 4x + 10y = 18 \end{cases}$

7. $\begin{cases} x - y = 0 \\ x + y = 2 \end{cases}$

8. $\begin{cases} x + 3y = -4 \\ y + x = 0 \end{cases}$

9. $\begin{cases} 3x - y = 17 \\ y + 2x = 8 \end{cases}$

10. Suppose your drama club is planning a production that will cost
$525 for the set and $150 per performance. A sold-out performance
will bring in $325. Write an equation for the cost C and an equation for
the income I for p sold-out performances. Find how many sold-out
performances will make the cost equal to the income.

Solve each system by substitution. Check your answers.

11. $\begin{cases} y = x + 1 \\ 2x + y = 7 \end{cases}$

12. $\begin{cases} x = y - 2 \\ 3x - y = 6 \end{cases}$

13. $\begin{cases} y = 2x + 3 \\ 5x - y = -3 \end{cases}$

14. $\begin{cases} 6x - 3y = -33 \\ 2x + y = -1 \end{cases}$

15. $\begin{cases} 2x - y = 7 \\ 3x - 2y = 10 \end{cases}$

16. $\begin{cases} 4x = 8y \\ 2x + 5y = 27 \end{cases}$

17. $\begin{cases} x + 3y = -4 \\ y + x = 0 \end{cases}$

18. $\begin{cases} 3x + 2y = 9 \\ x + y = 3 \end{cases}$

19. $\begin{cases} 2y - 3x = 4 \\ x = -4 \end{cases}$

20. Suppose you bought eight oranges and one grapefruit for a total of
$4.60. Later that day, you bought six oranges and three grapefruits for
a total of $4.80. Now you want to find the price of each orange and of
each grapefruit. Write an equation for each purchase. Solve the system
of equations.

Solve each system.

21. $\begin{cases} y = x + 3 \\ 5x + y = 9 \end{cases}$

22. $\begin{cases} 5x + 4y = 2 \\ -5x - 2y = 4 \end{cases}$

23. $\begin{cases} y = 2x + 3 \\ 5x - y = -3 \end{cases}$

24. $\begin{cases} 14x + 2y = 10 \\ x - 5y = 11 \end{cases}$

25. $\begin{cases} x + 5y = 1 \\ 2x = 2 - 10y \end{cases}$

26. $\begin{cases} 0.3x + 0.4y = 0.8 \\ 0.7x - 0.8y = -6.8 \end{cases}$

27. $\begin{cases} 4x + 3y = -6 \\ 5x - 6y = -27 \end{cases}$

28. $\begin{cases} 2y = -4x \\ 4x + 2y = -11 \end{cases}$

29. $\begin{cases} 1.2x + 1.4y = 2.7 \\ 0.4x - 0.3y = 0.9 \end{cases}$

Practice 3-3

Solving Systems of Inequalities

Solve each system of inequalities by graphing.

1. $\begin{cases} y > x + 2 \\ y \leq -x + 1 \end{cases}$

2. $\begin{cases} y \leq x + 3 \\ y \geq x + 2 \end{cases}$

3. $\begin{cases} x + y < 5 \\ y < 3x - 2 \end{cases}$

4. $\begin{cases} x - 2y < 3 \\ 2x + y > 8 \end{cases}$

5. $\begin{cases} -3x + y < 3 \\ x + y > -1 \end{cases}$

6. $\begin{cases} x + 2y > 4 \\ 2x - y > 6 \end{cases}$

7. $\begin{cases} 2x \geq y + 3 \\ x < 3 - 2y \end{cases}$

8. $\begin{cases} 3 < 2x - y \\ x - 3y \leq 4 \end{cases}$

9. $\begin{cases} y \geq 2 \\ y \geq |x| \end{cases}$

10. $\begin{cases} y < x - 3 \\ y \geq |x - 4| \end{cases}$

11. $\begin{cases} -2x + y > 1 \\ y > |x| \end{cases}$

12. $\begin{cases} y < -3 \\ y < -|x| \end{cases}$

13. Suppose you are buying two kinds of notebooks for school. A spiral notebook costs \$2, and a three-ring notebook costs \$5. You must have at least six notebooks. The cost of the notebooks can be no more than \$20.

    a. Write a system of inequalities to model the situation.

    b. Graph and solve the system.

14. A camp counselor needs no more than 30 campers to sign up for two mountain hikes. The counselor needs at least 10 campers on the low trail and at least 5 campers on the high trail.

    a. Write a system of inequalities to model the situation.

    b. Graph and solve the system.

Solve each system of inequalities by graphing.

15. $\begin{cases} 2x + y > 2 \\ x - y \geq 3 \end{cases}$

16. $\begin{cases} y \leq 3x \\ y \geq -2x + 2 \end{cases}$

17. $\begin{cases} y < 5x - 1 \\ y \geq 7 - 3x \end{cases}$

18. $\begin{cases} y \geq -2x + 2 \\ y \leq 3x \end{cases}$

19. $\begin{cases} x + y > 2 \\ 2x - y < 1 \end{cases}$

20. $\begin{cases} y > 3x + 2 \\ y \leq -2x + 1 \end{cases}$

21. $\begin{cases} y \geq -2 \\ y \leq -|x + 3| \end{cases}$

22. $\begin{cases} y < x + 3 \\ y > |x - 1| \end{cases}$

23. $\begin{cases} y > x \\ y < |x + 2| \end{cases}$

Practice 3-4

Linear Programming

Graph each system of constraints. Name all vertices. Then find the
values of *x* and *y* that maximize or minimize the objective function.

1. $\begin{cases} x + 2y \le 6 \\ x \ge 2 \\ y \ge 1 \end{cases}$

2. $\begin{cases} x + y \le 5 \\ x + 2y \le 8 \\ x \ge 0, y \ge 0 \end{cases}$

3. $\begin{cases} x + y \le 6 \\ 2x + y \le 10 \\ x \ge 0, y \ge 0 \end{cases}$

Minimum for
$C = 3x + 4y$

Maximum for
$P = x + 3y$

Maximum for
$P = 4x + y$

4. $\begin{cases} 3x + 2y \le 6 \\ 2x + 3y \le 6 \\ x \ge 0, y \ge 0 \end{cases}$

5. $\begin{cases} 4x + 2y \le 4 \\ 2x + 4y \le 4 \\ x \ge 0, y \ge 0 \end{cases}$

6. $\begin{cases} x + y \le 5 \\ 4x + y \le 8 \\ x \ge 0, y \ge 0 \end{cases}$

Maximum for
$P = 4x + y$

Maximum for
$P = 3x + y$

Minimum for
$C = x + 3y$

Find the values of *x* and *y* that maximize or minimize the objective
function for each graph. Then find the maximum or minimum value.

7.

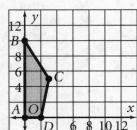

Maximize for $P = 2x + 3y$

8.

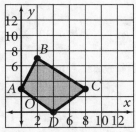

Minimize for $C = x + 2y$

9.

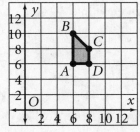

Maximize for $P = 3x + y$

10. You are going to make and sell bread. A loaf of Irish soda bread is
made with 2 c flour and $\frac{1}{4}$ c sugar. Kugelhopf cake is made with 4 c flour
and 1 c sugar. You will make a profit of $1.50 on each loaf of Irish soda
bread and a profit of $4 on each Kugelhopf cake. You have 16 c flour
and 3 c sugar.

   a. How many of each kind of bread should you make to maximize
   the profit?

   b. What is the maximum profit?

11. Suppose you make and sell skin lotion. A quart of regular skin lotion
contains 2 c oil and 1 c cocoa butter. A quart of extra-rich skin lotion
contains 1 c oil and 2 c cocoa butter. You will make a profit of $10/qt
on regular lotion and a profit of $8/qt on extra-rich lotion. You have
24 c oil and 18 c cocoa butter.

   a. How many quarts of each type of lotion should you make to
   maximize your profit?

   b. What is the maximum profit?

Practice 3-5

Describe the location of each point in coordinate space.

1. $(3, 0, 0)$ **2.** $(0, 2, 0)$ **3.** $(3, -2, -4)$ **4.** $(-6, -4, -1)$

5. $(0, 0, 4)$ **6.** $(1, 2, 3)$ **7.** $(3, -1, 6)$ **8.** $(0, 4, -1)$

Graph each point in coordinate space.

9. $(0, 3, 0)$ **10.** $(2, 0, 0)$ **11.** $(0, 0, 5)$ **12.** $(-1, -4, -2)$

13. $(2, 3, 1)$ **14.** $(-1, -2, -3)$ **15.** $(6, -1, 0)$ **16.** $(4, -2, 3)$

Write the coordinates of each point in the diagram.

17. A **18.** B

19. C **20.** D

21. R **22.** T

23. U **24.** S

Graph each equation.

25. $x + 2y + 3z = 3$ **26.** $3x - 2y + z = 6$

27. $-6x - 3y + 2z = 6$ **28.** $2x - 3y + 3z = 6$

29. $8x - 2y - 2z = 8$ **30.** $-6x - 12y - 12z = 12$

31. $9x - 3y + z = 9$ **32.** $7x - 1y + 7z = 7$

33. $4x + 3y + 6z = 12$ **34.** $x - y + 2z = 6$

Graph each equation and find the equation of each trace.

35. $x + y + z = 3$ **36.** $x + 2y + 3z = 6$ **37.** $x + 3y + 2z = 6$

38. $2x + 3y + z = 6$ **39.** $-4x + 2y - 4z = 8$ **40.** $4x - 2y + 6z = 12$

41. $6x - 3y + z = 6$ **42.** $7x - 3y + 7z = 21$ **43.** $4x - 3y + 6z = -12$

Practice 3-6

Systems with Three Variables

Solve each system.

1. $\begin{cases} x + y + z = -1 \\ 2x - y + 2z = -5 \\ -x + 2y - z = 4 \end{cases}$

2. $\begin{cases} x + y + z = 3 \\ 2x - y + 2z = 6 \\ 3x + 2y - z = 13 \end{cases}$

3. $\begin{cases} 2x + y = 9 \\ x - 2z = -3 \\ 2y + 3z = 15 \end{cases}$

4. $\begin{cases} x - y + 2z = 10 \\ -x + y - 2z = 5 \\ 3x - 3y + 6z = -2 \end{cases}$

5. $\begin{cases} 2x - y + z = -4 \\ 3x + y - 2z = 0 \\ 3x - y = -4 \end{cases}$

6. $\begin{cases} 2x - y - z = 4 \\ -x + 2y + z = 1 \\ 3x + y + z = 16 \end{cases}$

7. $\begin{cases} x + 5y + 5z = -10 \\ x + y + z = 2 \\ x + 2y + 3z = -3 \end{cases}$

8. $\begin{cases} x - y - z = 0 \\ x - 2y - 2z = 3 \\ -2x + 2y - z = 3 \end{cases}$

9. $\begin{cases} 3x + y + z = 6 \\ 3x - 2y + 2z = 14 \\ 3x + 3y - 3z = -6 \end{cases}$

10. $\begin{cases} x + y + z = -2 \\ 2x + 2y - 3z = 11 \\ 3x - y + z = 4 \end{cases}$

11. $\begin{cases} x - 5y + z = 3 \\ x + 2y - 2z = -12 \\ 2x + 2z = 6 \end{cases}$

12. $\begin{cases} 2x + 3z = 2 \\ 3x + 6y = 6 \\ x - 2z = 8 \end{cases}$

13. $\begin{cases} x + y - z = 0 \\ 3x - y + z = 4 \\ 5x + z = 7 \end{cases}$

14. $\begin{cases} x - 2y = 1 \\ x + 3y + z = 0 \\ 2x - 2z = 18 \end{cases}$

15. $\begin{cases} x + y + 4z = 5 \\ -2x + 2z = 3 \\ 3x + y - 2z = 0 \end{cases}$

16. $\begin{cases} 3x + 2y + 2z = 4 \\ -6x + 4y - 2z = -9 \\ 9x - 2y + 2z = 10 \end{cases}$

17. $\begin{cases} 2x - 3y + z = -3 \\ x - 5y + 7z = -11 \\ -10x + 4y - 6z = 28 \end{cases}$

18. $\begin{cases} x + y + z = -8 \\ x - y - z = 6 \\ 2x - 3y + 2z = -1 \end{cases}$

19. $\begin{cases} 14x - 3y + 5z = -15 \\ 3x + 2y - 6z = 10 \\ 7x - y + 4z = -5 \end{cases}$

20. $\begin{cases} 5x - 3y + 2z = 39 \\ 4x + 4y - 3z = 34 \\ 3x - 2y + 6z = 14 \end{cases}$

21. $\begin{cases} x + y + z = 6 \\ 2x - y + 2z = 6 \\ -x + y + 3z = 10 \end{cases}$

22. $\begin{cases} 2x + y - z = 3 \\ 3x - y + 3z = 3 \\ -x - 3y + 2z = 3 \end{cases}$

23. $\begin{cases} 2x - 3y + z = 4 \\ -2x + 3y - z = -4 \\ 6x - 9y + 3z = 12 \end{cases}$

24. $\begin{cases} x + y - z = 1 \\ x + 2z = 3 \\ 2x + 2y = 4 \end{cases}$

Write and solve a system of equations for each problem.

25. The sum of three numbers is −2. The sum of three times the first number, twice the second number, and the third number is 9. The difference between the second number and half the third number is 10. Find the numbers.

26. Monica has $1, $5, and $10 bills in her wallet that are worth $96. If she had one more $1 bill, she would have just as many $1 bills as $5 and $10 bills combined. She has 23 bills total. How many of each denomination does she have?

Practice 4-1

Organizing Data into Matrices

Write the dimensions of each matrix. Identify the indicated element.

1. $\begin{bmatrix} 2 \\ -3 \\ -6 \end{bmatrix}$; a_{21}

2. $\begin{bmatrix} 5 & -7 & 23 & 10 \\ -9 & 3 & 5 & -2 \\ 1 & 9 & 0 & 2 \end{bmatrix}$; a_{23}

3. $\begin{bmatrix} 2 & 3 & -9 \\ 12 & -8 & 0 \end{bmatrix}$; a_{21}

4. $\begin{bmatrix} x & y & z \\ a & b & c \\ p & q & r \end{bmatrix}$; a_{32}

5. $\begin{bmatrix} 2 & -2 \\ 3 & -3 \\ 4 & -4 \end{bmatrix}$; a_{31}

6. $\begin{bmatrix} 5 & 8 & -7 & -4 \end{bmatrix}$; a_{14}

Use the table for Exercises 7–10.

7. Display the data in a matrix with the types of unemployment in the columns.

8. State the dimensions of the matrix.

9. Identify a_{21}, and tell what it represents.

10. Identify a_{16}, and tell what it represents.

Unemployment by Category

	June, 1992	June, 1996
Construction	17.6%	9.5%
Manufacturing	8.3%	5.1%
Transportation	5.4%	4.5%
Sales	8.7%	6.4%
Finance	4.0%	2.6%
Services	6.6%	5.1%
Government	3.5%	2.7%

Source: *U.S. News & World Report*

Use the table at the right for Exercises 11–14.

11. Write a matrix M to represent the data in the graph, with columns representing years.

12. What are the dimensions of this matrix?

13. What does the first row represent?

14. What does m_{32} represent?

Days Lost to Strikes per 1,000 Employees

Source: *U.S. News & World Report*

Practice 4-2

Adding and Subtracting Matrices

Find the value of each variable.

1. $\begin{bmatrix} a & 2b \\ c-2 & d+3 \end{bmatrix} = \begin{bmatrix} 5 & -7 \\ 10 & 10 \end{bmatrix}$

2. $\begin{bmatrix} 3 & 5 & -y & x \\ z & 0 & 3a & b \end{bmatrix} = \begin{bmatrix} 3 & 3c & 7 & 4 \\ \frac{7}{2} & 0 & -9 & 3b \end{bmatrix}$

3. $\begin{bmatrix} 5 & 1 \\ 0 & 2 \end{bmatrix} + \begin{bmatrix} 2 & -13 \\ -10 & -10 \end{bmatrix} = \begin{bmatrix} 2x+1 & -4x \\ 5z & 2.5z-x \end{bmatrix}$

Use the information in the table.

4. Put the data in two matrices: one for males and one for females.

5. Use matrix subtraction to find the difference between the number of males and the number of females in each club each year.

Club Membership at TC High School

	1961–1962		2001–2002	
	Males	**Females**	**Males**	**Females**
Beta	37	23	56	58
Spanish	0	93	76	82
Chess	87	0	102	34
Library	6	18	27	29

Find each sum or difference.

6. $\begin{bmatrix} -1 & 2 \\ 3 & -1 \end{bmatrix} + \begin{bmatrix} -1 & 2 \\ -3 & 1 \end{bmatrix} + \begin{bmatrix} 0 & -1 \\ 2 & 0 \end{bmatrix}$

7. $\begin{bmatrix} 8 & -5 & -5 \\ 4 & -10 & 10 \\ 2 & -15 & -15 \end{bmatrix} - \begin{bmatrix} 0 & 0 & 1 \\ 1 & -2 & -2 \\ -2 & -3 & 3 \end{bmatrix}$

8. $\begin{bmatrix} -2 & -1 \\ -3 & 1 \\ -1 & -1 \end{bmatrix} - \begin{bmatrix} -2 & -2 \\ 3 & -1 \\ 0 & -2 \end{bmatrix} + \begin{bmatrix} -2 & 1 \\ 0 & 3 \\ -3 & -3 \end{bmatrix}$

9. $\begin{bmatrix} 1 \\ 1 \\ 1 \end{bmatrix} + \begin{bmatrix} -1 \\ -3 \\ 5 \end{bmatrix} + \begin{bmatrix} -10 \\ -7 \\ 11 \end{bmatrix} - \begin{bmatrix} -3 \\ -5 \\ -6 \end{bmatrix}$

Solve each matrix equation.

10. $X - \begin{bmatrix} 3 & 4 \\ 4 & 2 \\ 1 & 9 \end{bmatrix} = \begin{bmatrix} 5 & 7 \\ 9 & 12 \\ 3 & 2 \end{bmatrix}$

11. $X + \begin{bmatrix} 20 & -9 & -3 \\ 19 & -2 & -5 \\ -1 & 0 & -8 \end{bmatrix} = \begin{bmatrix} -7 & 92 & -5 \\ 0 & 91 & -6 \\ -9 & -1 & 12 \end{bmatrix}$

12. $\begin{bmatrix} -2 & -3 \\ 2 & 2 \end{bmatrix} = X - \begin{bmatrix} 1 & -1 \\ -2 & 2 \end{bmatrix}$

13. $\begin{bmatrix} 2 & 2 & 0 \\ 1 & -1 & -1 \end{bmatrix} = \begin{bmatrix} 2 & -2 & 3 \\ -3 & -3 & 4 \end{bmatrix} - X$

Determine whether the two matrices in each pair are equal.
Justify your reasoning.

14. $\begin{bmatrix} 2 \\ \sqrt{9} \\ 16 \end{bmatrix}; \begin{bmatrix} \frac{4}{2} & 3 & 4^2 \end{bmatrix}$

15. $\begin{bmatrix} 2(3) & 3(1.5) \\ 7 & \frac{10}{2} \end{bmatrix}; \begin{bmatrix} 6 & 4.5 \\ 7 & 5 \end{bmatrix}$

Practice 4-3

Matrix Multiplication

Use matrices A, B, C, D, and E to find each product, sum, or difference, if possible. If not possible, write *product undefined, sum undefined,* or *difference undefined.*

$$A = \begin{bmatrix} 1 & -1 \\ 3 & -2 \end{bmatrix} \qquad B = \begin{bmatrix} 0 & 2 \\ -2 & 1 \\ -1 & 0 \end{bmatrix} \qquad C = \begin{bmatrix} 3 & -3 & -1 \\ 2 & -2 & 4 \end{bmatrix} \qquad D = \begin{bmatrix} 1 & 0 \\ 0 & 1 \end{bmatrix} \qquad E = \begin{bmatrix} 3 \\ -3 \\ 2 \end{bmatrix}$$

1. $3AB$

2. $2A + 4D$

3. $5D - A$

4. $2C - E$

5. $3D + A$

6. DA

7. AE

8. BD

9. DB

10. CE

11. DC

12. EB

13. CB

14. $2D$

15. BE

16. $0.2B$

17. $\frac{1}{4}C$

18. $0.5AC$

19. DE

20. $-3DE$

Find the dimensions of the product matrix. Then find each product.

21. $\begin{bmatrix} 1 \\ 2 \\ 3 \end{bmatrix}\begin{bmatrix} 1 & 2 & 3 & 4 \end{bmatrix}$

22. $\begin{bmatrix} 1 & 2 & 12 \\ 12 & 2 & 1 \end{bmatrix}\begin{bmatrix} 3 & 4 \\ 4 & 3 \\ 5 & 2 \end{bmatrix}$

23. $\begin{bmatrix} 1 & 2 \\ 2 & 1 \end{bmatrix}\begin{bmatrix} 2 & 1 \\ 1 & 2 \end{bmatrix}$

Find each product if possible. If not possible, write *product undefined.*

24. $-12\begin{bmatrix} -6 & -2 \\ -5 & -6 \\ 0 & 1 \end{bmatrix}$

25. $\begin{bmatrix} 3 & 2 \\ 4 & 6 \\ 1 & 1 \end{bmatrix}\begin{bmatrix} -3 & 3 & -2 \\ -2 & 5 & -1 \end{bmatrix}$

26. $\begin{bmatrix} 0 & 1 & 0 \\ 2 & 2 & 1 \end{bmatrix}\begin{bmatrix} -2 & 2 & 2 \\ -1 & 1 & 1 \\ 0 & -1 & -1 \end{bmatrix}$

27. $\begin{bmatrix} 1 & 1 & 1 \\ 1 & 1 & 1 \\ 1 & 1 & 1 \end{bmatrix}\begin{bmatrix} 2 & 3 \\ 4 & 1 \\ 5 & 6 \end{bmatrix}$

28. $\begin{bmatrix} 1 & 0 & 1 \\ 1 & 1 & 0 \\ 1 & 1 & 1 \end{bmatrix}\begin{bmatrix} 6 & 4 & 2 & 8 \\ 10 & 4 & 6 & 2 \\ 2 & 10 & 12 & 4 \end{bmatrix}$

29. $\begin{bmatrix} 4 & 3 \\ 9 & 7 \end{bmatrix}\begin{bmatrix} 6 & 3 \\ 9 & 4 \end{bmatrix}$

Solve each equation. Check your answers.

30. $2\begin{bmatrix} 0 & 1 \\ 3 & -4 \end{bmatrix} - 3X = \begin{bmatrix} 9 & -6 \\ 1 & -2 \end{bmatrix}$

31. $\frac{1}{2}X + \begin{bmatrix} 5 & -1 \\ 0 & \frac{2}{3} \end{bmatrix} = 2\begin{bmatrix} 3 & 0 \\ 1 & 2 \end{bmatrix}$

Practice 4-4

Geometric Transformations with Matrices

For Exercises 1–11, use △ABC at the right. Find the coordinates of the image under each transformation. Express your answer as a matrix.

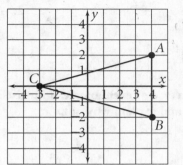

1. a dilation of 11

2. a translation 1 unit right and 4 units up

3. a dilation of 1.5

4. a translation 2 units right and 6 units down

5. a reflection in $y = x$

6. a rotation of 270°

7. a rotation of 90°

8. a translation 1 unit left and 2 units down

9. a translation 3 units left and 1 unit up

10. a dilation of $\frac{1}{2}$

11. a reflection in the x-axis

Graph each figure and its image after the given transformation.

12. $\begin{bmatrix} 2 & -3 & 6 & 4 \\ 0 & 1 & 1 & -4 \end{bmatrix}$; a dilation of 2

13. $\begin{bmatrix} 8 & 3 & -2 & -5 & 2 \\ 7 & 6 & 1 & 0 & -4 \end{bmatrix}$; a translation 2 units left and 1 unit up

14. $\begin{bmatrix} 2 & 4 & 5 & 3 \\ 1 & 1 & 3 & 5 \end{bmatrix}$; a translation 5 units left and 4 units down

15. $\begin{bmatrix} 2 & 1 & 6 & -4 \\ 0 & -3 & 5 & -2 \end{bmatrix}$; a rotation of 180°

16. $\begin{bmatrix} 6 & 5 & 1 & -3 & 6 \\ -1 & 6 & 2 & 0 & -4 \end{bmatrix}$; a reflection in the y-axis

The coordinates of the vertices of a polygon are given. Represent each transformation with matrices. Then express the coordinates of the vertices of the image as a matrix.

17. $I(21, -14), J(0, -7), K(-14, 0), L(0, 7)$; a dilation of $\frac{1}{7}$

18. $M(2, 0), N(0, -2), P(-2, 0)$; a translation 2 units down

19. $Q(2, 0), R(0, -2), S(-2, 0)$; a reflection in $y = -x$

Practice 4-5

Find the matrix E^{-1} for each.

1. $E = \begin{bmatrix} 2 & -2 \\ -1 & 2 \end{bmatrix}$

2. $E = \begin{bmatrix} 1 & -1 \\ 1 & 1 \end{bmatrix}$

3. $E = \begin{bmatrix} 2 & -1 \\ 1 & 0 \end{bmatrix}$

4. $E = \begin{bmatrix} 2 & 3 \\ 1 & 1 \end{bmatrix}$

5. $E = \begin{bmatrix} 1 & 4 \\ 1 & 3 \end{bmatrix}$

6. $E = \begin{bmatrix} 4 & 7 \\ 3 & 5 \end{bmatrix}$

Find the inverse of each matrix, if it exists. If it does not exist, write *no inverse* and explain why not.

7. $\begin{bmatrix} 3 & 4 \\ -3 & 4 \end{bmatrix}$

8. $\begin{bmatrix} 3 & 4 \\ 3 & 4 \end{bmatrix}$

9. $\begin{bmatrix} 1 & 2 \\ 3 & 4 \end{bmatrix}$

10. $\begin{bmatrix} 30 & -4 \\ -25 & 3 \end{bmatrix}$

Solve each matrix equation.

11. $\begin{bmatrix} 1 & 2 \\ -1 & -2 \end{bmatrix} X = \begin{bmatrix} 2 \\ -2 \end{bmatrix}$

12. $\begin{bmatrix} 1 & 1 \\ 1 & -1 \end{bmatrix} X = \begin{bmatrix} 3 \\ -1 \end{bmatrix}$

13. $\begin{bmatrix} -2 & 3 \\ -4 & 5 \end{bmatrix} X = \begin{bmatrix} 6 \\ 8 \end{bmatrix}$

Evaluate the determinant of each matrix.

14. $\begin{bmatrix} -3 & 4 \\ 1 & -1 \end{bmatrix}$

15. $\begin{bmatrix} 3 & 9 \\ 3 & 2 \end{bmatrix}$

16. $\begin{bmatrix} 1 & -4 \\ 2 & 6 \end{bmatrix}$

17. $\begin{bmatrix} 4 & -3 \\ 1 & -8 \end{bmatrix}$

18. $\begin{bmatrix} 5 & 4 \\ 4 & 5 \end{bmatrix}$

19. $\begin{bmatrix} 1 & -12 \\ 3 & 0 \end{bmatrix}$

Determine whether the matrices are multiplicative inverses.

20. $\begin{bmatrix} 2 & 1 \\ 5 & 3 \end{bmatrix}, \begin{bmatrix} 3 & -1 \\ -5 & 2 \end{bmatrix}$

21. $\begin{bmatrix} 4 & 9 \\ 2 & 6 \end{bmatrix}, \begin{bmatrix} 1 & -\frac{3}{2} \\ -\frac{1}{3} & \frac{2}{3} \end{bmatrix}$

22. $\begin{bmatrix} 1 & 2 \\ 3 & 4 \end{bmatrix}, \begin{bmatrix} -2 & 1 \\ \frac{3}{2} & -\frac{1}{2} \end{bmatrix}$

Practice 4-6

3 × 3 Matrices, Determinants, and Inverses

Where necessary, use a graphing calculator. Find the inverse (A^{-1}) of each matrix, if it exists. If it does not exist, write *no inverse*.

1. $\begin{bmatrix} 1 & 2 & 0 \\ -2 & 0 & -3 \\ 3 & -1 & 5 \end{bmatrix}$
2. $\begin{bmatrix} 1 & 1 & 1 \\ 2 & 1 & 0 \\ 0 & 2 & 3 \end{bmatrix}$
3. $\begin{bmatrix} 2 & 4 & 3 \\ 0 & 5 & -1 \\ 1 & -1 & 2 \end{bmatrix}$
4. $\begin{bmatrix} 0 & 2 & 0 \\ 2 & 0 & 2 \\ 0 & 2 & 0 \end{bmatrix}$

5. $\begin{bmatrix} 4 & 5 & 6 \\ 0 & 1 & 2 \\ 8 & 9 & 5 \end{bmatrix}$
6. $\begin{bmatrix} 1 & -1 & 1 \\ 0 & 0 & 0 \\ 0 & 0 & 1 \end{bmatrix}$
7. $\begin{bmatrix} -1 & 0 & -1 \\ 0 & -2 & 0 \\ -2 & 0 & 3 \end{bmatrix}$
8. $\begin{bmatrix} -3 & -2 & -1 \\ 0 & 1 & 2 \\ 3 & 4 & -4 \end{bmatrix}$

Solve each equation for X.

9. $\begin{bmatrix} 1 & 0 & 0 \\ 0 & 1 & 0 \\ 0 & 0 & 1 \end{bmatrix} X = \begin{bmatrix} 4 \\ -5 \\ 3 \end{bmatrix}$
10. $\begin{bmatrix} 1 & 2 & 0 \\ -2 & 0 & -3 \\ 3 & -1 & 5 \end{bmatrix} X = \begin{bmatrix} -1 \\ 12 \\ -20 \end{bmatrix}$
11. $\begin{bmatrix} 0 & 0 & 1 \\ 0 & 0 & 1 \\ 1 & 1 & 1 \end{bmatrix} X = \begin{bmatrix} 3 \\ 4 \\ 3 \end{bmatrix}$

Evaluate the determinant of each matrix.

12. $\begin{bmatrix} -1 & 2 & -2 \\ 0 & 1 & 3 \\ 4 & 2 & -1 \end{bmatrix}$
13. $\begin{bmatrix} 2 & 1 & 2 \\ -1 & 0 & 5 \\ 0 & 4 & 1 \end{bmatrix}$
14. $\begin{bmatrix} 2 & 4 & 3 \\ -3 & 0 & -2 \\ -1 & 3 & 0 \end{bmatrix}$

15. $\begin{bmatrix} 2 & 6 & -1 \\ 1 & 0 & 0 \\ 1 & 3 & -2 \end{bmatrix}$
16. $\begin{bmatrix} -4 & 0 & 3 \\ 0 & -2 & 3 \\ -1 & 4 & -2 \end{bmatrix}$
17. $\begin{bmatrix} 7 & -1 & 3 \\ 1 & 2 & 6 \\ 4 & 1 & 3 \end{bmatrix}$

Determine whether the matrices are multiplicative inverses.

18. $A = \begin{bmatrix} -2 & 2 & 3 \\ 1 & -1 & 0 \\ 0 & 1 & 4 \end{bmatrix}, B = \begin{bmatrix} -\frac{4}{3} & -\frac{5}{3} & 1 \\ -\frac{4}{3} & -\frac{8}{3} & 1 \\ 1 & \frac{2}{3} & 0 \end{bmatrix}$

19. $A = \begin{bmatrix} 2 & -17 & 11 \\ -1 & 11 & -7 \\ 0 & 3 & -2 \end{bmatrix}, B = \begin{bmatrix} 1 & 1 & 2 \\ 2 & 4 & -3 \\ 3 & 6 & -5 \end{bmatrix}$

Practice 4-7

Solve each system.

1. $\begin{cases} x + y + z = 0.621 \\ 3x - 3y + 2z = -0.007 \\ 4x + 5y - 10z = 1.804 \end{cases}$

2. $\begin{cases} 3x + 4y + 2z = 0.5 \\ 8x - 5y - 5z = 8.1 \\ 5x + 5y + 5z = 1 \end{cases}$

3. $\begin{cases} 5x - 4y + 3z = -30 \\ 18x - 2y - 19z = 103 \\ 2.9x + 0.06y + 17z = -81.8 \end{cases}$

4. $\begin{cases} x + 3y = 5 \\ x + 4y = 6 \end{cases}$

5. $\begin{cases} 4x + y + z = 0 \\ 5x + 2y + 3z = -15 \\ 6x - 5y - 5z = 52 \end{cases}$

6. $\begin{cases} 2x + 3y = 12 \\ x + 2y = 7 \end{cases}$

7. $\begin{cases} x + y + z = 31 \\ x - y + z = 1 \\ x - 2y + 2z = 7 \end{cases}$

8. $\begin{cases} x - 3y = -1 \\ -6x + 19y = 6 \end{cases}$

9. $\begin{cases} x + y + z = 8.8 \\ 2x - 5y + 9z = -4.8 \\ 3x + 2y - 7z = -7.6 \end{cases}$

10. $\begin{cases} -3x + 4y = 2 \\ x - y = -1 \end{cases}$

11. $\begin{cases} 0.5x + 1.5y + z = 7 \\ 3x + 3y + 5z = 3 \\ 2x + y + 2z = -1 \end{cases}$

12. $\begin{cases} x + y + z = -2 \\ 1.5x + 3y + 0.5z = 8 \\ 9x + 4y + 5z = 4 \end{cases}$

Write each system as a matrix equation. Identify the coefficient matrix, the variable matrix, and the constant matrix.

13. $\begin{cases} 6x + 9y = 36 \\ 4x + 13y = 2 \end{cases}$

14. $\begin{cases} 3x - 4y = -9 \\ 7y = 24 \end{cases}$

15. $\begin{cases} 4x - z = 9 \\ 12x + 2y = 17 \\ x - y + 12z = 3 \end{cases}$

Write a system of equations. Solve the system using an inverse matrix.

16. In 1992, there were 548,303 doctors under the age of 65 in the United States. Of those under age 45, 25.53415% were women. Of those between the ages of 45 and 64, 11.67209% were women. There were 110,017 women doctors under the age of 65. How many doctors were under age 45?

17. An apartment building has 50 units. All are one- or two-bedroom units. One-bedroom units rent for $425/mo, and two-bedroom units rent for $550/mo. When all units are occupied, the total monthly income is $25,000. How many apartments of each type are there?

Solve each matrix equation. If the coefficient matrix has no inverse, write *no unique solution.*

18. $\begin{bmatrix} 0.25 & -0.75 \\ 3.5 & 2.25 \end{bmatrix} \begin{bmatrix} x \\ y \end{bmatrix} = \begin{bmatrix} 1.5 \\ -3.75 \end{bmatrix}$

19. $\begin{bmatrix} 3 & -9 \\ 1 & -6 \end{bmatrix} \begin{bmatrix} a \\ b \end{bmatrix} = \begin{bmatrix} 12 \\ 0 \end{bmatrix}$

20. $\begin{bmatrix} 3 & -6 \\ -1 & 2 \end{bmatrix} \begin{bmatrix} u \\ v \end{bmatrix} = \begin{bmatrix} 4 \\ 9 \end{bmatrix}$

21. $\begin{bmatrix} 12 & -3 \\ 16 & 4 \end{bmatrix} \begin{bmatrix} x \\ y \end{bmatrix} = \begin{bmatrix} 144 \\ -64 \end{bmatrix}$

Determine whether each system has a unique solution.

22. $\begin{cases} 4d + 2e = 4 \\ d + 3e = 6 \end{cases}$

23. $\begin{cases} 3x - 2y = 43 \\ 9x - 6y = 40 \end{cases}$

24. $\begin{cases} -y - z = 3 \\ x + 2y + 3z = 1 \\ 4x - 5y - 6z = -50 \end{cases}$

Practice 4-8

Write a system of equations for each augmented matrix.

1. $\begin{bmatrix} 4 & -2 & | & 3 \\ 6 & 11 & | & 9 \end{bmatrix}$

2. $\begin{bmatrix} 12 & 6 & | & -4 \\ -1 & 0 & | & 2 \end{bmatrix}$

3. $\begin{bmatrix} -2 & 9 & -2 & | & 20 \\ 3 & -1 & 2 & | & 29 \\ 6 & 5 & 5 & | & -4 \end{bmatrix}$

Use Cramer's Rule to solve each system.

4. $\begin{cases} 2x + y = 1 \\ 3x - y = 9 \end{cases}$

5. $\begin{cases} 2x - y = 10 \\ x - 3y = 0 \end{cases}$

6. $\begin{cases} 3x + 5y = 1 \\ x + 6y = 9 \end{cases}$

7. $\begin{cases} x + y + z = 1.28 \\ x - 3y + 2z = 1.26 \\ 3x + 2y + 4z = 4.06 \end{cases}$

8. $\begin{cases} 2x + y - z = 0.75 \\ 3x + 3y + 2z = 4 \\ x - 5y + 3z = -2 \end{cases}$

9. $\begin{cases} x + y - z = 6 \\ 3x - 9y + z = -2 \\ 0.2x - 0.3y + 0.71z = -1.12 \end{cases}$

Write an augmented matrix for each system.

10. $\begin{cases} -3x + 4y = -8 \\ 2x - 8y = 16 \end{cases}$

11. $\begin{cases} u + 3v = -30 \\ 4u + v = 1 \end{cases}$

12. $\begin{cases} x - 4y + z = -9 \\ 3x + 2y - 3z = 9 \\ 4x + 2z = -4 \end{cases}$

Use an augmented matrix to solve each system.

13. $\begin{cases} x + y + z = 0 \\ 2x - 2y + 3z = 46 \\ 3x + 7y + 11z = 80 \end{cases}$

14. $\begin{cases} 3x + y + z = 18 \\ 4x + 2y + 3z = 12 \\ 7x + 8y + 5z = 9 \end{cases}$

15. $\begin{cases} 3x + 7y + 10z = 28 \\ 0.7x - 0.6y + 0.8z = 4.3 \\ 12x - 7y - 9z = 77 \end{cases}$

16. $\begin{cases} x - 2y - 3z = 2 \\ 2x + y - 5z = 30 \\ 7x - 11y - z = -48 \end{cases}$

17. $\begin{cases} x + y + z = 6.5 \\ 3x - 5y + 6z = -35 \\ 5x + 2y + 2z = 10 \end{cases}$

18. $\begin{cases} -x + y - z = -2 \\ 3x + 2y + 0.5z = -1.5 \\ 21x + 19y - 2z = -45 \end{cases}$

Use a graphing calculator to solve each system.

19. $\begin{cases} 4x - 2y + 3z = -2 \\ 2x + 2y + 5z = 16 \\ 8x - 5y - 2z = 4 \end{cases}$

20. $\begin{cases} x + y + z = -1 \\ 3x + 5y + 4z = 2 \\ 3x + 6y + 5z = 0 \end{cases}$

21. $\begin{cases} x + 3y - 2z = -3 \\ 2x + y - z = -6 \\ 3x - 2y + 4z = 8 \end{cases}$

Practice 5-1 **Modeling Data with Quadratic Functions**

Find a quadratic model for each set of values.

1. $(-1, 1), (1, 1), (3, 9)$

2. $(-4, 8), (-1, 5), (1, 13)$

3. $(-1, 10), (2, 4), (3, -6)$

4.
x	–1	0	2
$f(x)$	1	–1	7

5.
x	–4	0	1
$f(x)$	1	9	16

6.
x	–1	2	3
$f(x)$	12	3	4

Identify the vertex and the axis of symmetry of each parabola.

7.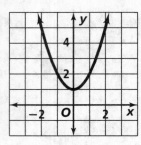

8.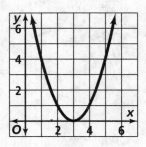

9.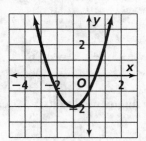

Determine whether each function is linear or quadratic. Identify the quadratic, linear, and constant terms.

10. $y = (x - 2)(x + 4)$

11. $y = 3x(x + 5)$

12. $y = 5x(x - 5) - 5x^2$

13. $f(x) = 7(x - 2) + 5(3x)$

14. $f(x) = 3x^2 - (4x - 8)$

15. $y = 3x(x - 1) - (3x + 7)$

16. $y = 3x^2 - 12$

17. $f(x) = (2x - 3)(x + 2)$

18. $y = 3x - 5$

For each parabola, identify points corresponding to P and Q.

19.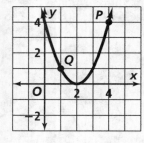

20.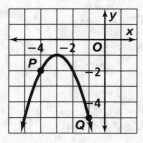

21.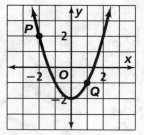

22. A toy rocket is shot upward from ground level. The table shows the height of the rocket at different times.

Time (seconds)	0	1	2	3	4
Height (feet)	0	256	480	672	832

  a. Find a quadratic model for this data.

  b. Use the model to estimate the height of the rocket after 1.5 seconds.

Practice 5-2

Graph each function. If $a > 0$, find the minimum value. If $a < 0$, find the maximum value.

1. $y = -x^2 + 2x + 3$ **2.** $y = 2x^2 + 4x - 3$ **3.** $y = -3x^2 + 4x$

4. $y = x^2 - 4x + 1$ **5.** $y = -x^2 - x + 1$ **6.** $y = 5x^2 - 3$

7. $y = \frac{1}{2}x^2 - x - 4$ **8.** $y = 5x^2 - 10x - 4$ **9.** $y = 3x^2 - 12x - 4$

Graph each function.

10. $y = x^2 + 3$ **11.** $y = x^2 - 4$ **12.** $y = x^2 + 2x + 1$

13. $y = 2x^2 - 1$ **14.** $y = -3x^2 + 12x - 8$ **15.** $y = \frac{1}{3}x^2 + 2x - 1$

16. Suppose you are tossing an apple up to a friend on a third-story balcony. After t seconds, the height of the apple in feet is given by $h = -16t^2 + 38.4t + 0.96$. Your friend catches the apple just as it reaches its highest point. How long does the apple take to reach your friend, and at what height above the ground does your friend catch it?

17. The barber's profit p each week depends on his charge c per haircut. It is modeled by the equation $p = -200c^2 + 2400c - 4700$. Sketch the graph of the equation. What price should he charge for the largest profit?

18. A skating rink manager finds that revenue R based on an hourly fee F for skating is represented by the function $R = -480F^2 + 3120F$. What hourly fee will produce maximum revenues?

19. The path of a baseball after it has been hit is modeled by the function $h = -0.0032d^2 + d + 3$, where h is the height in feet of the baseball and d is the distance in feet the baseball is from home plate. What is the maximum height reached by the baseball? How far is the baseball from home plate when it reaches it's maximum height?

20. A lighting fixture manufacturer has daily production costs of $C = 0.25n^2 - 10n + 800$, where C is the total daily cost in dollars and n is the number of light fixtures produced. How many fixtures should be produced to yield a minimum cost?

Graph each function. Label the vertex and the axis of symmetry.

21. $y = x^2 - 2x - 3$ **22.** $y = 2x - \frac{1}{4}x^2$ **23.** $y = x^2 + 6x + 7$

24. $y = x^2 + 2x - 6$ **25.** $y = x^2 - 8x$ **26.** $y = 2x^2 + 12x + 5$

27. $y = -3x^2 - 6x + 5$ **28.** $y = -2x^2 + 3$ **29.** $y = x^2 - 6$

Practice 5-3

Translating Parabolas

Write the equation of the parabola in vertex form.

1.
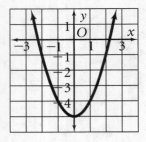

2.
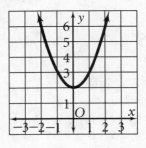

3.
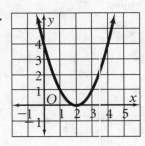

4.
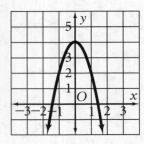

5.
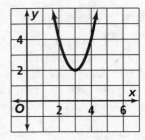

6.
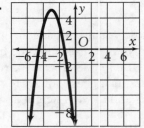

Graph each function.

7. $y = (x - 2)^2 - 3$

8. $y = (x - 6)^2 + 6$

9. $y = \frac{1}{2}(x - 1)^2 - 1$

10. $y = 8(x + 1)^2 - 2$

11. $y = -3(x - 1)^2 + 3$

12. $y = 3(x + 2)^2 + 4$

13. $y = \frac{1}{8}(x + 1)^2 - 1$

14. $y = \frac{1}{2}(x + 6)^2 - 2$

15. $y = 2(x + 3)^2 - 3$

16. $y = 4(x - 2)^2$

17. $y = -2(x + 1)^2 - 5$

18. $y = 4(x - 1)^2 - 2$

Write each function in vertex form.

19. $y = x^2 + 4x$

20. $y = 2x^2 + 8x + 3$

21. $y = -2x^2 - 8x$

22. $y = -x^2 + 4x + 4$

23. $y = x^2 - 4x - 4$

24. $y = x^2 + 5x$

25. $y = 2x^2 - 6$

26. $y = -3x^2 - x - 8$

27. $y = x^2 + 7x + 1$

28. $y = x^2 + 8x + 3$

29. $y = 2x^2 + 6x + 10$

30. $y = x^2 + 4x - 3$

Identify the vertex and the y-intercept of the graph of each function.

31. $y = 3(x - 2)^2 - 4$

32. $y = -\frac{1}{3}(x + 6)^2 + 5$

33. $y = 2(x - 1)^2 - 1$

34. $y = \frac{2}{3}(x + 4)^2 - 3$

35. $y = (x - 1)^2 + 2$

36. $y = -3(x - 2)^2 + 4$

37. $y = 4(x - 5)^2 + 1$

38. $y = -2(x + 5)^2 - 3$

39. $y = -5(x + 2)^2 + 5$

Practice 5-4

Factoring Quadratic Expressions

Factor each expression completely.

1. $x^2 + 4x + 4$

2. $x^2 - 7x + 10$

3. $x^2 + 7x - 8$

4. $x^2 - 6x$

5. $2x^2 - 9x + 4$

6. $x^2 + 2x - 35$

7. $x^2 + 6x + 5$

8. $x^2 - 9$

9. $x^2 - 13x - 48$

10. $x^2 - 4$

11. $4x^2 + x$

12. $x^2 - 29x + 100$

13. $x^2 - x - 6$

14. $9x^2 - 1$

15. $3x^2 - 2x$

16. $x^2 - 64$

17. $x^2 - 25$

18. $x^2 - 81$

19. $x^2 - 36$

20. $x^2 - 100$

21. $x^2 - 1$

22. $4x^2 - 1$

23. $4x^2 - 36$

24. $9x^2 - 4$

25. $x^2 - 7x - 8$

26. $x^2 + 13x + 36$

27. $x^2 - 5x + 6$

28. $x^2 + 5x + 4$

29. $x^2 - 21x - 22$

30. $x^2 + 13x + 40$

31. $2x^2 - 5x - 3$

32. $x^2 + 10x - 11$

33. $x^2 - 14x + 24$

34. $5x^2 + 4x - 12$

35. $2x^2 - 5x - 7$

36. $2x^2 + 13x + 15$

37. $3x^2 - 7x - 6$

38. $3x^2 + 16x + 21$

39. $x^2 + 5x - 24$

40. $x^2 + 34x - 72$

41. $x^2 - 11x$

42. $3x^2 + 21x$

43. $x^2 + 8x + 12$

44. $x^2 - 10x + 24$

45. $x^2 + 7x - 30$

46. $x^2 - 2x - 168$

47. $x^2 - x - 72$

48. $4x^2 - 25$

49. $x^2 - 121$

50. $x^2 + 17x + 16$

51. $10x^2 - 17x + 3$

52. $4x^2 + 12x + 9$

53. $4x^2 - 4x - 15$

54. $9x^2 - 4$

55. $x^2 + 6x - 40$

56. $2x^2 - 8$

57. $x^2 + 18x + 77$

58. $2x^2 - 98$

59. $x^2 + 21x + 98$

60. $x^2 + 20x + 84$

61. $9x^2 + 30x + 16$

62. $8x^2 - 6x - 27$

63. $x^2 - 3x - 54$

64. $x^2 - 169$

65. $25x^2 - 9$

66. $7x^2 + 49$

67. $2x^2 - 10x - 28$

68. $x^2 + 8x + 12$

69. $x^2 - 2x - 35$

70. $x^2 + 2x - 63$

71. $20x^2 - 11x - 3$

72. $12x^2 + 4x - 5$

73. $4x^2 - 5x - 6$

74. $8x^2 + 22x - 21$

75. $3x^2 - 3x - 168$

Practice 5-5

Solve each equation by factoring, by taking square roots, or by graphing.
When necessary, round your answer to the nearest hundredth.

1. $x^2 - 18x - 40 = 0$

2. $16x^2 = 56x$

3. $5x^2 = 15x$

4. $x^2 - 6x - 7 = 0$

5. $x^2 - 49 = 0$

6. $x^2 + 2x + 1 = 0$

7. $x^2 - 1 = 0$

8. $x^2 - 3x - 4 = 0$

9. $x^2 + 9x^2 + 20 = 0$

10. $6x^2 + 9 = -55x$

11. $(x + 5)^2 = 36$

12. $2x^2 - 3x = 0$

13. $2x^2 + x - 10 = 0$

14. $-4x^2 + 3x = -1$

15. $5x^2 - 6x + 1 = 0$

16. $3x^2 + 1 = -4x$

17. $-2x^2 + 2 = -3x$

18. $6x^2 + 1 = 5x$

19. $-2x^2 - x + 1 = 0$

20. $3x^2 + 5x = 2$

21. $x^2 - 6x = -8$

22. $x^2 + 6 = -7x$

23. $6x^2 + 18x = 0$

24. $2x^2 + 5 = 11x$

25. $3x^2 - 7x + 2 = 0$

26. $2x^2 - 3x = -1$

27. $2x^2 - x = 6$

28. $x^2 - 144 = 0$

29. $4x^2 + 2 = 6x$

30. $5x^2 + 2 = -7x$

31. $7x^2 + 6x - 1 = 0$

32. $2x^2 - 6x = -4$

33. $11x^2 - 12x + 1 = 0$

34. $7x^2 + 1 = -8x$

35. $x^2 + 9 = -10x$

36. $(x - 2)^2 = 18$

37. $x^2 - 8x + 7 = 0$

38. $x^2 - 16 = 0$

39. $x^2 + 6x = -8$

40. $x^2 + 3 = 4x$

41. $2x^2 + 6 = -7x$

42. $6x^2 + 2 = 7x$

43. $(x + 7)^2 = \frac{49}{16}$

44. $9x^2 - 8x = 1$

45. $10x^2 + 7x + 1 = 0$

46. $4x^2 + 2 = -9x$

47. $3x^2 + 4 = 8x$

48. $4x^2 + 5 + 9x = 0$

49. $9x^2 + 10x = -1$

50. $2x^2 + 9x + 4 = 0$

51. $2x^2 + 6x = -4$

52. $11x^2 - 1 = -10x$

53. $4x^2 = 1$

54. $6x^2 = 12x$

55. $25x^2 - 9 = 0$

56. $2x^2 + 11x = 6$

57. $8x^2 - 6x + 1 = 0$

58. $x^2 + 11 = -12x$

59. $6x^2 + 2 = 13x$

60. $x^2 = 121$

61. $4x^2 - 11x = 3$

62. $8x^2 + 6x + 1 = 0$

63. $x^2 + 9x + 8 = 0$

64. $x^2 + 8x = -12$

65. $x^2 + 6x = 40$

66. $2x^2 = 8$

67. $x^2 = x + 6$

68. $x^2 + 2x - 6 = 0$

69. $x^2 - 12 = 0$

70. $3x^2 + 4x = 6$

71. $7x^2 - 105 = 0$

72. $16x^2 = 81$

73. $x^2 + 5x + 4 = 0$

74. $x^2 + 36 = -13x$

75. $x^2 + 6 = 5x$

Practice 5-6

Find the first three output values for each function. Use $z = 0$ for the first input value.

1. $f(z) = z^2 + 2i$

2. $f(z) = z^2 + 1 + i$

Find the additive inverse of each of the following.

3. $2 + 3i$ **4.** $-4 + i$ **5.** $2i$ **6.** $-1 - i$

7. $-6i$ **8.** $5 - 2i$ **9.** $-2 + 3i$ **10.** 4

Find each absolute value.

11. $|-2i|$ **12.** $|5 + 12i|$ **13.** $|-1 - i|$ **14.** $|2 + i|$ **15.** $|4 + 3i|$

16. $|5 - 2i|$ **17.** $|3 - 2i|$ **18.** $|-2 + i|$ **19.** $|3 - 3i|$ **20.** $|3i|$

21. $|2i|$ **22.** $|4 + i|$ **23.** $|6 - 3i|$ **24.** $|-3 + i|$ **25.** $|4|$

Simplify each expression.

26. $\sqrt{40}$ **27.** $\sqrt{-88}$ **28.** $-\sqrt{-36}$

29. $(1 + 5i) + (1 - 5i)$ **30.** $(3 + 2i) - (3 + 2i)$ **31.** $4 - \sqrt{-25}$

32. $(2 + 6i) - (7 + 9i)$ **33.** $(1 + 5i)(1 - 5i)$ **34.** $(1 + 5i)(6 - 3i)$

35. $(5 - 6i)(6 - 2i)$ **36.** $(3 + 4i)(3 + 4i)$ **37.** $(2 + 3i)(2 - 3i)$

38. $(2 + 2i)(2 - 2i)$ **39.** $(-3 - 2i)(1 - 3i)$ **40.** $(3 + 3i) - (4 - 3i)$

41. $\sqrt{-48}$ **42.** $\sqrt{-300}$ **43.** $\sqrt{-75}$

44. $\sqrt{-16} + 2$ **45.** $(4 - i)(4 - i)$ **46.** $(4 + 2i)(1 - 7i)$

47. $(1 + 3i)(1 - 7i)$ **48.** $(2 + 4i)(-3 - 2i)$ **49.** $(11 - 12i)(11 + 12i)$

50. $(2 + 3i) + (-4 + 5i)$ **51.** $(5 + 14i) - (10 - 2i)$ **52.** $(5 + 12i)(5 - 12i)$

53. $(3 + 4i)(1 - 2i)$ **54.** $(6 + 2i)(1 - 2i)$ **55.** $(5 - 13i)(5 - 13i)$

56. $\sqrt{-44}$ **57.** $-\sqrt{-63}$ **58.** $\sqrt{-8}$

59. $(2 + 3i)(4 + 5i)$ **60.** $(5 + 4i) - (-1 - 2i)$ **61.** $(1 + 2i)(-1 - 2i)$

62. $(-1 + 4i)(1 - 2i)$ **63.** $(6 + 2i) + (1 - 2i)$ **64.** $(3 + 2i)(3 + 2i)$

65. $(-2 + 3i) + (4 + 5i)$ **66.** $(5 + 4i)(1 + 2i)$ **67.** $(-1 - 5i)(-1 + 5i)$

Solve each equation.

68. $x^2 + 80 = 0$ **69.** $5x^2 + 500 = 0$ **70.** $2x^2 + 40 = 0$ **71.** $3x^2 + 36 = 0$

72. $3x^2 + 75 = 0$ **73.** $2x^2 + 144 = 0$ **74.** $4x^2 + 1600 = 0$ **75.** $4x^2 + 1 = 0$

76. $2x^2 + 10 = 0$ **77.** $4x^2 + 100 = 0$ **78.** $x^2 + 9 = 0$ **79.** $9x^2 + 90 = 0$

Practice 5-7

Complete the square.

1. $x^2 + 6x + \blacksquare$ **2.** $x^2 - 7x + \blacksquare$ **3.** $x^2 + 12x + \blacksquare$ **4.** $x^2 + 3x + \blacksquare$

5. $x^2 - 8x + \blacksquare$ **6.** $x^2 + 16x + \blacksquare$ **7.** $x^2 + 21x + \blacksquare$ **8.** $x^2 - 2x + \blacksquare$

Rewrite each equation in vertex form. Then find the vertex.

9. $y = x^2 + 4x - 6$ **10.** $y = x^2 - 6x + 6$ **11.** $y = 4x^2 + 8x - 4$

12. $y = 4x^2 + 4x + 1$ **13.** $y = 2x^2 + 4x - 5$ **14.** $y = -3x^2 - 4x - 1$

15. $y = -3x^2 + 3x - 1$ **16.** $y = x^2 + 2x + 1$ **17.** $y = -5x^2 + 10x + 1$

18. $y = -2x^2 + 4x + 3$ **19.** $y = x^2 + 5x + \frac{5}{4}$ **20.** $y = -2x^2 + 10x - 11$

21. $y = 6x^2 - 12x + 1$ **22.** $y = -2x^2 + 8x - 9$ **23.** $y = 3x^2 + 9x + 6$

Solve each quadratic equation by completing the square.

24. $x^2 + 12x + 4 = 0$ **25.** $x^2 - x - 5 = 0$ **26.** $3x^2 = -12x - 3$

27. $x^2 - x - 1 = 0$ **28.** $4x^2 - 8x + 1 = 0$ **29.** $5x^2 = 8x - 6$

30. $2x^2 - 4x - 3 = 0$ **31.** $x^2 + 11x = 0$ **32.** $x^2 = 5x + 14$

33. $2x^2 + x - 1 = 0$ **34.** $2x^2 + 6x - 7 = 0$ **35.** $2x^2 = -8x + 45$

36. $x^2 = -3x - 3$ **37.** $4x^2 = -2x + 1$ **38.** $3x^2 = -6x + 9$

39. $x^2 = 7x + 12$ **40.** $x^2 = 3x + 7$ **41.** $3x^2 = 6x - 9$

42. $x^2 = -3x + 2$ **43.** $x^2 = -7x - 1$ **44.** $4x^2 = -3x + 2$

45. $2x^2 = 4x - 5$ **46.** $2x^2 = 5x + 5$ **47.** $2x^2 = 6x + 5$

48. $x^2 = 3x$ **49.** $x^2 = 8x$ **50.** $4x^2 = -2x - 3$

51. $2x^2 = -2x + 5$ **52.** $2x^2 = -5x - 5$ **53.** $3x^2 = -5x + 1$

54. $2x^2 = 2x + 4$ **55.** $3x^2 = 7x + 8$ **56.** $2x^2 = -6x + 4$

57. $x^2 = -7x - 9$ **58.** $2x^2 = 5x$ **59.** $3x^2 = -42x$

60. $2x^2 = -4x + 5$ **61.** $4x^2 = -x + 5$ **62.** $3x^2 = -3x + 1$

63. $x^2 = 3x + 4$ **64.** $2x^2 = 2x + 8$ **65.** $3x^2 = x + 4$

Solve each equation.

66. $x^2 + 2x + 1 = 9$ **67.** $3x^2 - 18x + 27 = 125$ **68.** $x^2 - 4x + 4 = 5$

69. $x^2 + 3x + \frac{9}{4} = \frac{13}{4}$ **70.** $x^2 + 3x + \frac{9}{4} = -\frac{15}{4}$ **71.** $x^2 + 3x + \frac{9}{4} = \frac{41}{4}$

72. $x^2 + 7x + \frac{49}{4} = \frac{53}{4}$ **73.** $x^2 + 3x + \frac{9}{4} = \frac{29}{4}$ **74.** $x^2 - 6x + 9 = 7$

Practice 5-8

Evaluate the discriminant of each equation. Tell how many solutions each equation has and whether the solutions are real or imaginary.

1. $y = x^2 + 10x - 25$ **2.** $y = x^2 + 10x + 10$ **3.** $y = 9x^2 - 24x$

4. $y = 4x^2 - 4x + 1$ **5.** $y = 4x^2 - 5x + 1$ **6.** $y = 4x^2 - 3x + 1$

7. $y = x^2 + 3x + 4$ **8.** $y = x^2 + 7x - 3$ **9.** $y = -2x^2 + 3x - 5$

10. $y = x^2 - 5x + 4$ **11.** $y = x^2 + 12x + 36$ **12.** $y = x^2 + 2x + 3$

13. $y = 2x^2 - 13x - 7$ **14.** $y = -5x^2 + 6x - 4$ **15.** $y = -4x^2 - 4x - 1$

Solve each equation using the Quadratic Formula.

16. $x^2 + 6x + 9 = 0$ **17.** $x^2 - 15x + 56 = 0$ **18.** $3x^2 - 5x + 2 = 0$

19. $2x^2 + 3x + 5 = 0$ **20.** $10x^2 - 23x + 12 = 0$ **21.** $4x^2 + x - 5 = 0$

22. $x^2 + 8x + 15 = 0$ **23.** $3x^2 + 2x + 1 = 0$ **24.** $4x^2 + x + 5 = 0$

25. $x^2 - 4x - 12 = 0$ **26.** $x^2 = 3x + 2$ **27.** $2x^2 - 5x + 2 = 0$

28. $x^2 + 6x - 4 = 0$ **29.** $x^2 = 2x - 5$ **30.** $3x^2 + 7 = -6x$

31. $2x^2 + 6x + 3 = 0$ **32.** $x^2 = -18x - 80$ **33.** $x^2 + 9x - 13 = 0$

34. $x^2 - 8x + 25 = 0$ **35.** $4x^2 + 13x = 12$ **36.** $3x^2 - 5x = -12$

37. $3x^2 + 4x + 5 = 0$ **38.** $2x^2 = 3x - 7$ **39.** $5x^2 + 2x + 1 = 0$

40. $5x^2 + x + 3 = 0$ **41.** $5x^2 + x = 3$ **42.** $5x^2 - 2x + 7 = 0$

43. $x^2 - 2x + 3 = 0$ **44.** $-2x^2 + 3x = 24$ **45.** $4x^2 = 5x - 6$

46. $x^2 + 6x + 5 = 0$ **47.** $x^2 - 6x = -8$ **48.** $x^2 - 6x = -6$

Solve.

49. A model of the daily profits p of a gas station based on the price per gallon g is $p = -15,000g^2 + 34,500g - 16,800$. Use the discriminant to find whether the station can profit $4000 per day. Explain.

Solve each equation using the Quadratic Formula. Find the exact solutions. Then approximate any radical solutions. Round to the nearest hundredth.

50. $x^2 - 2x - 3 = 0$ **51.** $x^2 + 5x + 4 = 0$ **52.** $x^2 - 2x - 8 = 0$

53. $7x^2 - 12x + 3 = 0$ **54.** $5x^2 + 5x - 1 = 0$ **55.** $4x^2 + 5x + 1 = 0$

56. $6x^2 + 5x - 4 = 0$ **57.** $x^2 + x = 6$ **58.** $x^2 - 13x = 48$

59. $2x^2 + 5x = 0$ **60.** $x^2 + 3x - 3 = 0$ **61.** $x^2 - 4x + 1 = 0$

62. $9x^2 - 6x - 7 = 0$ **63.** $x^2 - 35 = 2x$ **64.** $x^2 + 7x + 10 = 0$

Practice 6-1

Polynomial Functions

Find a cubic model for each function. Then use your model to estimate the value of y when $x = 7$.

1.

x	0	2	4	6	8	10
y	25	21	20	23	19	17

2.

x	0	2	4	6	8	10
y	3.1	4.2	4.3	4.4	5.1	6.7

Write each polynomial in standard form. Then classify it by degree and by number of terms.

3. $4x + x + 2$

4. $-3 + 3x - 3x$

5. $6x^4 - 1$

6. $1 - 2s + 5s^4$

7. $5m^2 - 3m^2$

8. $x^2 + 3x - 4x^3$

9. $-1 + 2x^2$

10. $5m^2 - 3m^3$

11. $5x - 7x^2$

12. $2 + 3x^3 - 2$

13. $6 - 2x^3 - 4 + x^3$

14. $6x - 7x$

15. $a^3(a^2 + a + 1)$

16. $x(x + 5) - 5(x + 5)$

17. $p(p - 5) + 6$

18. $(3c^2)^2$

19. $-(3 - b)$

20. $6(2x - 1)$

21. $\frac{2}{3} + s^2$

22. $\frac{2x^4 + 4x - 5}{4}$

23. $\frac{3 - z^5}{3}$

24. The lengths of the sides of a triangle are $x + 4$ units, x units, and $x + 1$ units. Express the perimeter of the triangle as a polynomial in standard form.

25. Find a cubic function to model the data below. (Hint: Use the number of years past 1940 for x.) Then use the function to estimate the average monthly Social Security Benefit for a retired worker in 2005.

Average Monthly Social Security Benefits, 1940–1999

Year	1940	1950	1960	1970	1980	1990	1999
Amount (in dollars)	22.71	29.03	81.73	123.82	321.10	550.50	757.71

Source: *www.infoplease.com*

26. Find a cubic function to model the data below. (Hint: Use x to represent the gestation period.) Then use the function to estimate the longevity of an animal with a gestation period of 151 days.

Gestation and Longevity of Certain Animals

Animal	Rat	Squirrel	Pig	Cow	Elephant
Gestation (in days)	21	44	115	280	624
Longevity (in years)	3	9	10	12	40

Source: *www.infoplease.com*

Practice 6-2

For each function, determine the zeros. State the multiplicity of any multiple zeros.

1. $y = (x - 5)^3$

2. $y = x(x - 8)^2$

3. $y = (x - 2)(x + 7)^3$

4. $f(x) = x^4 - 8x^3 + 16x^2$

5. $f(x) = 9x^3 - 81x$

6. $y = (2x + 5)(x - 3)^2$

Write each function in standard form.

7. $y = (x - 5)(x + 5)(2x - 1)$

8. $y = (2x + 1)(x - 3)(5 - x)$

9. A rectangular box is 24 in. long, 12 in. wide, and 18 in. high. If each dimension is increased by x in., write a polynomial function in standard form modeling the volume V of the box.

Write a polynomial function in standard form with the given zeros.

10. $-1, 3, 4$

11. $1, 1, 2$

12. $-3, 0, 0, 5$

13. -2 multiplicity 3

Write each expression as a polynomial in standard form.

14. $x(x - 1)^2$

15. $(x + 3)^2(x + 1)$

16. $(x + 4)(2x - 5)(x + 5)^2$

Write each function in factored form. Check by multiplication.

17. $y = 2x^3 + 10x^2 + 12x$

18. $y = x^4 - x^3 - 6x^2$

19. $y = -3x^3 + 18x^2 - 27x$

Find the zeros of each function. Then graph the function.

20. $y = (x + 1)(x - 1)(x - 3)$

21. $y = (x + 2)(x - 3)$

22. $y = x(x - 2)(x + 5)$

Find the relative maximum, relative minimum, and zeros of each function.

23. $f(x) = x^3 - 7x^2 + 10x$

24. $f(x) = x^3 - x^2 - 9x + 9$

Write each polynomial in factored form. Check by multiplication.

25. $x^3 - 6x^2 - 16x$

26. $x^3 + 7x^2 + 12x$

27. $x^3 - 8x^2 + 15x$

28. A rectangular box has a square base. The combined length of a side of the square base, and the height is 20 in. Let x be the length of a side of the base of the box.

    a. Write a polynomial function in factored form modeling the volume V of the box.

    b. What is the maximum possible volume of the box?

Practice 6-3

Determine whether each binomial is a factor of $x^3 + 3x^2 - 10x - 24$.

1. $x + 4$ **2.** $x - 3$ **3.** $x + 6$ **4.** $x + 2$

Divide using synthetic division.

5. $(x^3 - 8x^2 + 17x - 10) \div (x - 5)$

6. $(x^3 + 5x^2 - x - 9) \div (x + 2)$

7. $(-2x^3 + 15x^2 - 22x - 15) \div (x - 3)$

8. $(x^3 + 7x^2 + 15x + 9) \div (x + 1)$

9. $(x^3 + 2x^2 + 5x + 12) \div (x + 3)$

10. $(x^3 - 5x^2 - 7x + 25) \div (x - 5)$

11. $(x^4 - x^3 + x^2 - x + 1) \div (x - 1)$

12. $\left(x^4 + \frac{5}{3}x^3 - \frac{2}{3}x^2 + 6x - 2 \right) \div \left(x - \frac{1}{3} \right)$

13. $(x^4 - 5x^3 + 5x^2 + 7x - 12) \div (x - 4)$

14. $(2x^4 + 23x^3 + 60x^2 - 125x - 500) \div (x + 4)$

Use synthetic division and the Remainder Theorem to find $P(a)$.

15. $P(x) = 3x^3 - 4x^2 - 5x + 1; a = 2$

16. $P(x) = x^3 + 7x^2 + 12x - 3; a = -5$

17. $P(x) = x^3 + 6x^2 + 10x + 3; a = -3$

18. $P(x) = 2x^4 - 9x^3 + 7x^2 - 5x + 11; a = 4$

Divide using long division. Check your answers.

19. $(x^2 - 13x - 48) \div (x + 3)$

20. $(2x^2 + x - 7) \div (x - 5)$

21. $(x^3 + 5x^2 - 3x - 1) \div (x - 1)$

22. $(3x^3 - x^2 - 7x + 6) \div (x + 2)$

Use synthetic division and the given factor to completely factor each polynomial function.

23. $y = x^3 + 3x^2 - 13x - 15; (x + 5)$

24. $y = x^3 - 3x^2 - 10x + 24; (x - 2)$

Divide.

25. $(6x^3 + 2x^2 - 11x + 12) \div (3x + 4)$

26. $(x^4 + 2x^3 + x - 3) \div (x - 1)$

27. $(2x^4 + 3x^3 - 4x^2 + x + 1) \div (2x - 1)$

28. $(x^5 - 1) \div (x - 1)$

29. $(x^4 - 3x^2 - 10) \div (x - 2)$

30. $(3x^3 - 2x^2 + 2x + 1) \div \left(x + \frac{1}{3} \right)$

31. A box is to be mailed. The volume in cubic inches of the box can be expressed as the product of its three dimensions: $V(x) = x^3 - 16x^2 + 79x - 120$. The length is $x - 8$. Find linear expressions for the other dimensions. Assume that the width is greater than the height.

Practice 6-4

Solving Polynomial Equations

• •

Factor the expression on the left side of each equation. Then solve the equation.

1. $8x^3 - 27 = 0$

2. $x^3 + 64 = 0$

3. $2x^3 + 54 = 0$

4. $2x^3 - 250 = 0$

5. $4x^3 - 32 = 0$

6. $27x^3 + 1 = 0$

7. $64x^3 - 1 = 0$

8. $x^3 - 27 = 0$

9. $x^4 - 5x^2 + 4 = 0$

10. $x^4 - 12x^2 + 11 = 0$

11. $x^4 - 10x^2 + 16 = 0$

12. $x^4 - 8x^2 + 16 = 0$

13. $x^4 - 9x^2 + 14 = 0$

14. $x^4 + 13x^2 + 36 = 0$

15. $x^4 - 10x^2 + 9 = 0$

16. $x^4 + 3x^2 - 4 = 0$

17. Over 3 yr, Lucia saved $550, $600, and $650 from baby-sitting jobs. The polynomial $550x^3 + 600x^2 + 650x$ represents her savings, with interest, after 3 yr. The annual interest rate equals $x - 1$. Find the interest needed so that she will have $2000 after 3 yr.

Solve each equation by graphing. Where necessary, round to the nearest hundredth.

18. $2x^4 = 9x^2 - 4$

19. $x^2 - 16x = -1$

20. $6x^3 + 10x^2 + 5x = 0$

21. $36x^3 + 6x^2 = 9x$

22. $15x^4 = 11x^3 + 14x^2$

23. $x^4 = 81x^2$

24. The product of three consecutives integers $n - 1, n$, and $n + 1$ is -336. Write and solve an equation to find the numbers.

Factor each expression.

25. $x^3 - 125$

26. $x^4 - 8x^2 + 15$

27. $x^4 + x^2 - 2$

28. $x^3 + 1$

29. $x^4 - 2x^2 - 24$

30. $x^4 + 10x^2 + 9$

31. $x^3 + 27$

32. $x^4 + 7x^2 - 18$

Solve each equation.

33. $x^4 - x = 0$

34. $3x^4 + 18 = 21x^2$

35. $2x^4 - 26x^2 - 28 = 0$

36. $5x^4 + 50x^2 + 80 = 0$

37. $x^4 - 81 = 0$

38. $x^4 = 25$

39. $x^5 = x^3 + 12x$

40. $x^4 + 12x^2 = 8x^3$

Practice 6-5

Theorems about Roots of Polynomial Equations

A polynomial equation with rational coefficients has the given roots. Find two additional roots.

1. $2 + 3i$ and $\sqrt{7}$

2. $3 - \sqrt{2}$ and $1 + \sqrt{3}$

3. $-4i$ and $6 - i$

4. $5 - \sqrt{6}$ and $-2 + \sqrt{10}$

Find a fourth-degree polynomial equation with integer coefficients that has the given numbers as roots.

5. $2i$ and $4 - i$

6. $\sqrt{2}$ and $2 - \sqrt{3}$

7. $3i$ and $\sqrt{6}$

8. $2 + i$ and $1 - \sqrt{5}$

Find the roots of each polynomial equation.

9. $x^3 - 5x^2 + 2x + 8 = 0$

10. $x^3 + x^2 - 17x + 15 = 0$

11. $2x^3 + 13x^2 + 17x - 12 = 0$

12. $x^3 - x^2 - 34x - 56 = 0$

13. $x^3 - 18x + 27 = 0$

14. $x^4 - 5x^2 + 4 = 0$

15. $x^3 - 6x^2 + 13x - 10 = 0$

16. $x^3 - 5x^2 + 4x + 10 = 0$

17. $x^3 - 5x^2 + 17x - 13 = 0$

18. $x^3 + x + 10 = 0$

19. $x^3 - 5x^2 - x + 5 = 0$

20. $x^3 - 12x + 16 = 0$

21. $x^3 - 2x^2 - 5x + 6 = 0$

22. $x^3 - 8x^2 - 200 = 0$

23. $x^3 + x^2 - 5x + 3 = 0$

24. $4x^3 - 12x^2 - x + 3 = 0$

25. $x^3 + x^2 - 7x + 2 = 0$

26. $12x^3 + 31x^2 - 17x - 6 = 0$

Use the Rational Root Theorem to list all possible rational roots for each polynomial equation. Then find any actual rational roots.

27. $x^3 + 5x^2 - 2x - 15 = 0$

28. $36x^3 + 144x^2 - x - 4 = 0$

29. $2x^3 + 5x^2 + 4x + 1 = 0$

30. $12x^4 + 14x^3 - 5x^2 - 14x - 4 = 0$

31. $5x^3 - 11x^2 + 7x - 1 = 0$

32. $x^3 + 81x^2 - 49x - 49 = 0$

Find a third-degree polynomial equation with rational coefficients that has the given numbers as roots.

33. $3, 2 - i$

34. $5, 2i$

35. $-1, 3 + i$

36. $-7, i$

37. $-4, 4i$

38. $6, 3 - 2i$

Practice 6-6

The Fundamental Theorem of Algebra

Find all the zeros of each function.

1. $y = 5x^3 - 5x$

2. $f(x) = x^3 - 16x$

3. $g(x) = 12x^3 - 2x^2 - 2x$

4. $y = 6x^3 + x^2 - x$

5. $f(x) = 5x^3 + 6x^2 + x$

6. $y = -4x^3 + 100x$

For each equation, state the number of complex roots, the possible number of real roots, and the possible rational roots.

7. $2x^2 + 5x + 3 = 0$

8. $3x^2 + 11x - 10 = 0$

9. $2x^4 - 18x^2 + 5 = 0$

10. $4x^3 - 12x + 9 = 0$

11. $6x^5 - 28x + 15 = 0$

12. $x^3 - x^2 - 2x + 7 = 0$

13. $x^3 - 6x^2 - 7x - 12 = 0$

14. $2x^4 + x^2 - x + 6 = 0$

15. $4x^5 - 5x^4 + x^3 - 2x^2 + 2x - 6 = 0$

16. $7x^6 + 3x^4 - 9x^2 + 18 = 0$

17. $5 + x + x^2 + x^3 + x^4 + x^5 = 0$

18. $6 - x + 2x^3 - x^3 + x^4 - 8x^5 = 0$

Find all the zeros of each function.

19. $f(x) = x^3 - 9x^2 + 27x - 27$

20. $y = 2x^3 - 8x^2 + 18x - 72$

21. $y = x^3 - 10x - 12$

22. $y = x^3 - 4x^2 + 8$

23. $f(x) = 2x^3 + x - 3$

24. $y = x^3 - 2x^2 - 11x + 12$

25. $g(x) = x^3 + 4x^2 + 7x + 28$

26. $f(x) = x^3 + 3x^2 + 6x + 4$

27. $g(x) = x^4 - 5x^2 - 36$

28. $y = x^4 - 7x^2 + 12$

29. $y = 9x^4 + 5x^2 - 4$

30. $y = 4x^4 - 11x^2 - 3$

Practice 6-7

Indicate whether each situation involves a combination or a permutation.

1. Five apples chosen at random from a case of apples.

2. Ten applicants line up for a job interview.

3. Three students elected president, secretary, and treasurer of the student body.

4. Four students chosen at random from the student body.

Evaluate each expression.

5. $_{12}C_{11}$ **6.** $_{12}C_{10}$ **7.** $_{12}C_5$ **8.** $_{12}C_1$

9. $_{12}C_{12}$ **10.** $_5C_4 + {_5C_3}$ **11.** $\dfrac{_5C_3}{_5C_2}$ **12.** $4(_7C_2)$

How many combinations of five can you make from each set?

13. Xul, Ben, Sue, Tom, and Ria   **14.** $\{0, 1, 2, 3, 4, 5, 6, 7, 8, 9\}$

15. 14 novels on a reading list   **16.** 50 states

Evaluate each expression.

17. $8!$ **18.** $\dfrac{11!}{9!}$ **19.** $6!4!$ **20.** $3(5!)$

21. $_{12}P_{11}$ **22.** $_{12}P_{10}$ **23.** $_{12}P_5$ **24.** $_{12}P_1$

25. In how many ways can four distinct positions for a relay race be assigned from a team of nine runners?

26. A committee must choose 3 finalists from 15 scholarship candidates. How many ways can the committee choose the three finalists?

27. A traveler can choose from three airlines, five hotels, and four rental car companies. How many arrangements of these services are possible?

28. In how many ways can four students be seated at a table with six chairs?

Assume a and b are positive integers. Decide whether each statement is true or false. If it is true, explain why. If it is false, give a counterexample.

29. $a!b! = b!a!$ **30.** $(a^2)! = (a!)^2$ **31.** $a \cdot b! = (ab)!$

32. $(a + 0)! = a!$ **33.** $(a + b)! = a! + b!$ **34.** $(a!)! = (a!)^2$

Practice 6-8

Use the Binomial Theorem to expand each binomial.

1. $(x + 2)^4$

2. $(a + 2)^7$

3. $(x + y)^7$

4. $(d - 2)^9$

5. $(2x - 3)^8$

6. $(x - 1)^9$

7. $(2x^2 - 2y^2)^6$

8. $(x^5 + 2y)^7$

9. What is the probability that you will roll exactly five sixes in ten tosses of a number cube?

10. One airline recently had a rate of 52 complaints per 100,000 departures, or a 0.00052 probability of a complaint on each flight.

    a. What is the probability that the airline will not have a complaint in 20 flights?

    b. What is the probability that the airline will not have a complaint in 100 flights?

    c. What is the probability that the airline will have a complaint in 100 flights?

11. 6% of the circuit boards assembled at a certain production plant are defective. If five circuit boards are chosen at random, what is the probability that exactly two are defective?

12. The probability that a baby will be a boy is $\frac{1}{2}$. What is the probability that a family with five children has all boys?

13. Your friend's batting average is 0.225. What is the probability of her getting three or more hits in the next five times at bat?

14. If a classmate randomly guesses on ten multiple choice questions, what is the probability that six or more answers will be right? The probability of each answer being correct is 0.2.

Use Pascal's Triangle to expand each binomial.

15. $(n - 3)^3$

16. $(2n + 2)^4$

17. $(n - 6)^5$

18. $(n - 1)^6$

19. $(2a + 2)^3$

20. $(x^2 - y^2)^4$

21. $(2x + 3y)^5$

22. $(2x^2 + y^2)^6$

23. $(x^2 - y^2)^3$

24. $(2b + c)^4$

25. $(3m - 2n)^5$

26. $(x^3 - y^4)^6$

Expand each binomial.

27. $(x + 1)^7$

28. $(x + 4)^8$

29. $(x - 3y)^6$

30. $(x + 2)^5$

31. $(x^2 - y^2)^5$

32. $(3 + y)^5$

33. $(x^2 + 3)^6$

34. $(x - 5)^7$

35. $(x - 4y)^4$

Practice 7-1

Roots and Radical Expressions

Find each real-number root.

1. $\sqrt{144}$

2. $-\sqrt{25}$

3. $\sqrt{-0.01}$

4. $\sqrt[3]{0.001}$

5. $\sqrt[4]{0.0081}$

6. $\sqrt[3]{27}$

7. $\sqrt[3]{-27}$

8. $\sqrt{0.09}$

Find all the real cube roots of each number.

9. 216

10. -343

11. -0.064

12. $\frac{1000}{27}$

Find all the real square roots of each number.

13. 400

14. -196

15. 10,000

16. 0.0625

Find all the real fourth roots of each number.

17. -81

18. 256

19. 0.0001

20. 625

Simplify each radical expression. Use absolute value symbols when needed.

21. $\sqrt{81x^4}$

22. $\sqrt{121y^{10}}$

23. $\sqrt[3]{8g^6}$

24. $\sqrt[3]{125x^9}$

25. $\sqrt[5]{243x^5y^{15}}$

26. $\sqrt[3]{(x-9)^3}$

27. $\sqrt{25(x+2)^4}$

28. $\sqrt[3]{\frac{64x^9}{343}}$

Find the two real-number solutions of each equation.

29. $x^2 = 4$

30. $x^4 = 81$

31. $x^2 = 0.16$

32. $x^2 = \frac{16}{49}$

33. A cube has volume $V = s^3$, where s is the length of a side. Find the side length for a cube with volume 8000 cm^3.

34. The velocity of a falling object can be found using the formula $v^2 = 64h$, where v is the velocity (in feet per second) and h is the distance the object has already fallen.

   a. What is the velocity of the object after a 10-foot fall?

   b. How much does the velocity increase if the object falls 20 feet rather than 10 feet?

Practice 7-2

Multiply and simplify. Assume that all variables are positive.

1. $\sqrt{4} \cdot \sqrt{6}$

2. $\sqrt{9x^2} \cdot \sqrt{9y^5}$

3. $\sqrt[3]{50x^2z^5} \cdot \sqrt[3]{15y^3z}$

4. $4\sqrt{2x} \cdot 3\sqrt{8x}$

5. $\sqrt{xy} \cdot \sqrt{4xy}$

6. $9\sqrt{2} \cdot 3\sqrt{y}$

Rationalize the denominator of each expression. Assume that all variables are positive.

7. $\sqrt{\dfrac{9x}{2}}$

8. $\dfrac{\sqrt{xy}}{\sqrt{3x}}$

9. $\sqrt[3]{\dfrac{x^2}{3y}}$

10. $\dfrac{\sqrt[4]{2x}}{\sqrt[4]{3x^2}}$

11. $\sqrt{\dfrac{x}{8y}}$

12. $\sqrt[3]{\dfrac{3a}{4b^2c}}$

Multiply. Simplify if possible. Assume that all variables are positive.

13. $\sqrt{4} \cdot \sqrt{25}$

14. $\sqrt{81} \cdot \sqrt{36}$

15. $\sqrt{3} \cdot \sqrt{27}$

16. $\sqrt[3]{-3} \cdot \sqrt[3]{9}$

17. $\sqrt{3x} \cdot \sqrt{6x^3}$

18. $\sqrt[3]{2xy^2} \cdot \sqrt[3]{4x^2y^7}$

Simplify. Assume that all variables are positive.

19. $\sqrt{36x^3}$

20. $\sqrt[3]{125y^2z^4}$

21. $\sqrt{18k^6}$

22. $\sqrt[3]{-16a^{12}}$

23. $\sqrt{x^2y^{10}z}$

24. $\sqrt[4]{256s^7t^{12}}$

25. $\sqrt[3]{216x^4y^3}$

26. $\sqrt{75r^3}$

27. $\sqrt[4]{625u^5v^8}$

Divide and simplify. Assume that all variables are positive.

28. $\dfrac{\sqrt{6x}}{\sqrt{3x}}$

29. $\dfrac{\sqrt[3]{4x^2}}{\sqrt[3]{x}}$

30. $\sqrt[4]{\dfrac{243k^3}{3k^7}}$

31. $\dfrac{\sqrt{(2x)^2}}{\sqrt{(5y)^4}}$

32. $\dfrac{\sqrt[3]{18y^2}}{\sqrt[3]{12y}}$

33. $\sqrt{\dfrac{162a}{6a^3}}$

34. The volume of a sphere of radius r is $V = \dfrac{4}{3}\pi r^3$.

    a. Use the formula to find r in terms of V. Rationalize the denominator.

    b. Use your answer to part (a) to find the radius of a sphere with volume 100 cubic inches. Round to the nearest hundredth.

Practice 7-3

Binomial Radical Expressions

Multiply each pair of conjugates.

1. $\left(3\sqrt{2} - 9\right)\left(3\sqrt{2} + 9\right)$

2. $\left(1 - \sqrt{7}\right)\left(1 + \sqrt{7}\right)$

3. $\left(5\sqrt{3} + \sqrt{2}\right)\left(5\sqrt{3} - \sqrt{2}\right)$

Add or subtract if possible.

4. $9\sqrt{3} + 2\sqrt{3}$

5. $5\sqrt{2} + 2\sqrt{3}$

6. $3\sqrt{7} - 7\sqrt[3]{x}$

7. $14\sqrt[3]{xy} - 3\sqrt[3]{xy}$

Rationalize each denominator. Simplify the answer.

8. $\dfrac{2}{2\sqrt{3} - 4}$

9. $\dfrac{5}{2 + \sqrt{3}}$

10. $\dfrac{1 + \sqrt{5}}{1 - \sqrt{5}}$

11. $\dfrac{2 + \sqrt{12}}{5 - \sqrt{12}}$

Simplify.

12. $3\sqrt{32} + 2\sqrt{50}$

13. $\sqrt{200} - \sqrt{72}$

14. $\sqrt[3]{81} - 3\sqrt[3]{3}$

15. $2\sqrt[4]{48} + 3\sqrt[4]{243}$

Multiply.

16. $\left(1 - \sqrt{5}\right)\left(2 + \sqrt{5}\right)$

17. $\left(1 + 4\sqrt{10}\right)\left(2 - \sqrt{10}\right)$

18. $\left(1 - 3\sqrt{7}\right)\left(4 - 3\sqrt{7}\right)$

19. $\left(4 - 2\sqrt{3}\right)^2$

20. $\left(\sqrt{2} + \sqrt{7}\right)^2$

21. $\left(2\sqrt{3} + 3\sqrt{2}\right)^2$

Simplify. Rationalize all denominators. Assume that all variables are positive.

22. $\sqrt{28} + 4\sqrt{63} - 2\sqrt{7}$

23. $6\sqrt{40} - 2\sqrt{90} + 3\sqrt{160}$

24. $3\sqrt{12} + 7\sqrt{75} - \sqrt{54}$

25. $4\sqrt[3]{81} + 2\sqrt[3]{72} - 3\sqrt[3]{24}$

26. $3\sqrt{225x} + 5\sqrt{144x}$

27. $6\sqrt{45y^2} + 4\sqrt{20y^2}$

28. $\left(3\sqrt{y} - \sqrt{5}\right)\left(2\sqrt{y} + 5\sqrt{5}\right)$

29. $\left(\sqrt{x} - \sqrt{3}\right)\left(\sqrt{x} + \sqrt{3}\right)$

30. $\dfrac{3 - \sqrt{10}}{\sqrt{5} - \sqrt{2}}$

31. $\dfrac{2 + \sqrt{14}}{\sqrt{7} + \sqrt{2}}$

32. $\dfrac{2 + \sqrt[3]{x}}{\sqrt[3]{x}}$

33. A park in the shape of a triangle has a sidewalk dividing it into two parts.

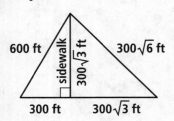

a. If a man walks around the perimeter of the park, how far will he walk?

b. What is the area of the park?

Practice 7-4

Rational Exponents

Simplify each expression. Assume that all variables are positive.

1. $27^{\frac{1}{3}}$

2. $\left(81^{\frac{1}{4}}\right)^4$

3. $\left(32^{\frac{1}{5}}\right)^5$

4. $(256^4)^{\frac{1}{4}}$

5. 7^0

6. $8^{\frac{2}{3}}$

7. $(-1)^{\frac{1}{5}}$

8. $(-27)^{\frac{2}{3}}$

9. $16^{\frac{1}{4}}$

10. $x^{\frac{1}{2}} \cdot x^{\frac{1}{3}}$

11. $2y^{\frac{1}{2}} \cdot y$

12. $(8^2)^{\frac{1}{3}}$

13. 3.6^0

14. $\left(\frac{1}{16}\right)^{\frac{1}{4}}$

15. $\left(\frac{27}{8}\right)^{\frac{2}{3}}$

16. $\sqrt[8]{0}$

17. $\left(3x^{\frac{1}{2}}\right)\left(4x^{\frac{2}{3}}\right)$

18. $\dfrac{12y^{\frac{1}{3}}}{4y^{\frac{1}{2}}}$

19. $\left(3a^{\frac{1}{2}}b^{\frac{1}{3}}\right)^2$

20. $\left(y^{\frac{2}{3}}\right)^{-9}$

21. $\left(a^{\frac{2}{3}}b^{-\frac{1}{2}}\right)^{-6}$

22. $y^{\frac{2}{5}} \cdot y^{\frac{3}{8}}$

23. $\left(\dfrac{x^{\frac{4}{7}}}{x^{\frac{2}{3}}}\right)$

24. $\left(2a^{\frac{1}{4}}\right)^3$

25. $81^{-\frac{1}{2}}$

26. $\left(2x^{\frac{2}{5}}\right)\left(6x^{\frac{1}{4}}\right)$

27. $\left(9x^4y^{-2}\right)^{\frac{1}{2}}$

28. The interest rate r required to increase your investment p to the amount a in t years is found by $r = \left(\dfrac{a}{p}\right)^{\frac{1}{t}} - 1$. What interest rate would be required to increase your investment of \$2700 to \$3600 over three years? Round your answer to the nearest tenth of a percent.

Write each expression in radical form.

29. $x^{\frac{4}{3}}$

30. $(2y)^{\frac{1}{3}}$

31. $a^{1.5}$

32. $b^{\frac{1}{5}}$

33. $z^{\frac{2}{3}}$

34. $(ab)^{\frac{1}{4}}$

35. $m^{2.4}$

36. $t^{-\frac{2}{7}}$

37. $a^{-1.6}$

Write each expression in exponential form.

38. $\sqrt{x^3}$

39. $\sqrt[3]{m}$

40. $\sqrt{5y}$

41. $\sqrt[3]{2y^2}$

42. $\left(\sqrt[4]{b}\right)^3$

43. $\sqrt{-6}$

44. $\sqrt{(6a)^4}$

45. $\sqrt[5]{n^4}$

46. $\sqrt[4]{(5ab)^3}$

Practice 7-5

Solve. Check for extraneous solutions.

1. $(x - 2)^{\frac{1}{3}} = 5$

2. $3x^{\frac{4}{3}} + 5 = 53$

3. $4x^{\frac{3}{2}} - 5 = 103$

4. $\sqrt{x + 1} = x - 1$

5. $\sqrt{2x + 1} = -3$

6. $x^{\frac{1}{2}} - 5 = 0$

7. $\sqrt{x + 7} = x - 5$

8. $(2x + 1)^{\frac{1}{3}} = -3$

9. $2x^{\frac{1}{3}} - 2 = 0$

10. $\sqrt{2x - 5} = 7$

11. $\sqrt{2x - 4} = x - 2$

12. $\sqrt{x} + 6 = x$

13. $\sqrt{x + 2} = 10 - x$

14. $\sqrt{4x + 2} = \sqrt{3x + 4}$

15. $(7x - 3)^{\frac{1}{2}} = 5$

16. $(x - 2)^{\frac{2}{3}} - 4 = 5$

17. $2\sqrt{x - 1} = \sqrt{26 + x}$

18. $2x^{\frac{3}{4}} = 16$

19. $\sqrt{7x - 6} - \sqrt{5x + 2} = 0$

20. $\sqrt{3x - 3} - 6 = 0$

21. $5\sqrt{x} + 2 = 12$

22. $2x^{\frac{4}{3}} - 2 = 160$

23. $4x^{\frac{1}{2}} - 5 = 27$

24. $\sqrt{x + 1} = x + 1$

25. $\sqrt{2x + 1} = -5$

26. $x^{\frac{1}{6}} - 2 = 0$

27. $\sqrt{x + 2} = x - 18$

28. $(2x + 1)^{\frac{1}{3}} = 1$

29. $x^{\frac{1}{4}} + 3 = 0$

30. $\sqrt[3]{2x - 4} = -2$

31. $x^{\frac{1}{4}} - 1 = 0$

32. $(x - 2)^{\frac{1}{3}} = -5$

33. $x^{\frac{1}{3}} - 2 = 0$

34. $\sqrt{3x} = 6$

35. $(2x + 7)^{\frac{1}{2}} - x = 2$

36. $\sqrt{4x} - 8 = 0$

37. $\sqrt{3x + 1} - 5 = 0$

38. $3(2x + 4)^{\frac{4}{3}} = 48$

39. $2\sqrt{x} = \sqrt{x + 6}$

40. $(2x + 1)^{\frac{1}{2}} = (5 - 2x)^{\frac{1}{2}}$

41. $(x + 14)^{\frac{1}{4}} = (2x)^{\frac{1}{2}}$

42. $\sqrt[3]{x - 2} = 4$

Practice 7-6

Function Operations

• •

1. A boutique prices merchandise by adding 80% to its cost. It later decreases by 25% the price of items that don't sell quickly.

   a. Write a function $f(x)$ to represent the price after the 80% markup.

   b. Write a function $g(x)$ to represent the price after the 25% markdown.

   c. Use a composition function to find the price of an item after both price adjustments that originally costs the boutique $150.

   d. Does the order in which the adjustments are applied make a difference? Explain.

Let $f(x) = 4x - 1$ and $g(x) = 2x^2 + 3$. Perform each function operation and then find the domain.

2. $f(x) + g(x)$ 3. $f(x) - g(x)$ 4. $f(x) \cdot g(x)$

5. $\dfrac{f(x)}{g(x)}$ 6. $g(x) - f(x)$ 7. $\dfrac{g(x)}{f(x)}$

Let $f(x) = -3x + 2$, $g(x) = \dfrac{x}{5}$, $h(x) = -2x^2 + 9$, and $j(x) = 5 - x$. Find each value or expression.

8. $(f \circ j)(3)$ 9. $(j \circ h)(-1)$ 10. $(h \circ g)(-5)$

11. $(g \circ f)(a)$ 12. $f(x) + j(x)$ 13. $f(x) - h(x)$

14. $(g \circ f)(-5)$ 15. $(f \circ g)(-2)$ 16. $3f(x) + 5g(x)$

17. $g(f(2))$ 18. $g(f(x))$ 19. $f(g(1))$

Let $g(x) = x^2 - 5$ and $h(x) = 3x + 2$. Perform each function operation.

20. $(h \circ g)(x)$ 21. $g(x) \cdot h(x)$ 22. $-2g(x) + h(x)$

23. A department store has marked down its merchandise by 25%. It later decreases by $5 the price of items that have not sold.

   a. Write a function $f(x)$ to represent the price after the 25% markdown.

   b. Write a function $g(x)$ to represent the price after the $5 markdown.

   c. Use a composition function to find the price of a $50 item after both price adjustments.

   d. Does the order in which the adjustments are applied make a difference? Explain.

• •

Practice 7-7

Graph each relation and its inverse.

1. $y = \dfrac{x + 3}{3}$

2. $y = \dfrac{1}{2}x + 5$

3. $y = 2x + 5$

4. $y = 4x^2$

5. $y = \dfrac{1}{2}x^2$

6. $y = \dfrac{2}{3}x^2$

Find the inverse of each function. Is the inverse a function?

7. $y = x^2 + 2$

8. $y = x + 2$

9. $y = 3(x + 1)$

10. $y = -x^2 - 3$

11. $y = 2x - 1$

12. $y = 1 - 3x^2$

13. $y = 5x^2$

14. $y = (x + 3)^2$

15. $y = 6x^2 - 4$

16. $y = 3x^2 - 2$

17. $y = (x + 4)^2 - 4$

18. $y = -x^2 + 4$

For each function f, find f^{-1} and the domain and range of f and f^{-1}. Determine whether f^{-1} is a function.

19. $f(x) = \dfrac{1}{6}x$

20. $f(x) = -\dfrac{1}{5}x + 2$

21. $f(x) = x^2 - 2$

22. $f(x) = x^2 + 4$

23. $f(x) = \sqrt{x - 1}$

24. $f(x) = \sqrt{3x}$

Find the inverse of each relation. Graph the given relation and its inverse.

25.

x	−2	−1	0	1
y	−3	−2	−1	0

26.

x	0	1	2	3
y	−3	−1	0	−2

Let $f(x) = 2x + 5$. Find each value.

27. $(f^{-1} \circ f)(-1)$

28. $(f \circ f^{-1})(3)$

29. $(f \circ f^{-1})\left(-\dfrac{1}{2}\right)$

30. The equation $f(x) = 198{,}900x + 635{,}600$ can be used to model the number of utility trucks under 6000 pounds that are sold each year in the U.S. with $x = 0$ representing the year 1992. Find the inverse of the function. Use the inverse to estimate in which year the number of utility trucks under 6000 pounds sold in the U.S. will be 4,000,000.
Source: *www.infoplease.com*

Practice 7-8

Graph each function.

1. $y = -\sqrt{x + 2}$

2. $y = \sqrt{x - 3}$

3. $y = \sqrt{x} + 1$

4. $y = -\sqrt{x} - 1$

5. $y = \sqrt{x - 4} + 2$

6. $y = \sqrt{x + 1} - 3$

7. $y = \sqrt{x + 2} - 6$

8. $y = -\sqrt{x - 2} + 3$

9. $y = -\sqrt{x - 3} + 3$

10. $y = \sqrt{x + 3} - 2$

11. $y = \sqrt{x - 1} - 5$

12. $y = -\sqrt{x - 2} + 5$

13. $y = -\sqrt{x + 1} - 4$

14. $y = -\sqrt{x - 1} + 2$

15. $y = \sqrt{x - 1} + 3$

16. $y = \sqrt{x - 2} + 1$

17. $y = \sqrt{x + 2} - 2$

18. $y = \sqrt{x - 1} + 2$

19. $y = \sqrt{x + 1} + 4$

20. $y = \sqrt{x - 3} + 3$

21. $y = \sqrt{x + 1} - 2$

22. $y = \sqrt{x - 1} - 1$

23. $y = \sqrt{x + 3} - 3$

24. $y = \sqrt{x + 4} - 1$

25. $y = \sqrt{x - 2} - 4$

26. $y = \sqrt{x + 2} + 1$

27. $y = \sqrt{x - 2} + 3$

28. If you know the area A of a circle, you can use the equation $r = \sqrt{\dfrac{A}{\pi}}$ to find the radius r.

   a. Graph the equation.

   b. What is the radius of a circle with an area of 350 ft^2?

Rewrite each function to make it easy to graph using a translation. Describe the graph.

29. $y = \sqrt{81x + 162}$

30. $y = -\sqrt{4x + 20}$

31. $y = \sqrt[3]{125x - 250}$

32. $y = -\sqrt{64x + 192}$

33. $y = -\sqrt[3]{8x - 56} + 4$

34. $y = \sqrt{25x + 75} - 1$

Graph each function.

35. $y = \sqrt[3]{x} - 1$

36. $y = \sqrt[3]{x + 2} - 3$

37. $y = \sqrt[3]{x + 1} - 2$

38. $y = -\sqrt[3]{x} + 2$

39. $y = 2\sqrt[3]{x - 3}$

40. $y = \sqrt[3]{x + 3} - 1$

Practice 8-1

Without graphing, determine whether each equation represents exponential growth or exponential decay.

1. $y = 72(1.6)^x$ **2.** $y = 24(0.8)^x$ **3.** $y = 3\left(\dfrac{6}{5}\right)^x$ **4.** $y = 7\left(\dfrac{2}{3}\right)^x$

Sketch the graph of each function. Identify the horizontal asymptote.

5. $y = (0.3)^x$ **6.** $y = 3^x$ **7.** $y = 2\left(\dfrac{1}{5}\right)^x$ **8.** $y = \dfrac{1}{2}(3)^x$

9. A new car that sells for $18,000 depreciates 25% each year. Write a function that models the value of the car. Find the value of the car after 4 yr.

10. A new truck that sells for $29,000 depreciates 12% each year. Write a function that models the value of the truck. Find the value of the truck after 7 yr.

11. The bear population increases at a rate of 2% per year. There are 1573 bear this year. Write a function that models the bear population. How many bears will there be in 10 yr?

12. An investment of $75,000 increases at a rate of 12.5% per year. Find the value of the investment after 30 yr.

13. The population of an endangered bird is decreasing at a rate of 0.75% per year. There are currently about 200,000 of these birds. Write a function that models the bird population. How many birds will there be in 100 yr?

Write an exponential function $y = ab^x$ for a graph that includes the given points.

14. $(0, 2), (1, 1.3)$ **15.** $(-1, 12.5), (4, 4.096)$ **16.** $(1, 0.84), (2, 1.008)$

For each annual rate of change, find the corresponding growth or decay factor.

17. $+45\%$ **18.** -10% **19.** -40% **20.** $+200\%$

For each function, find the annual percent increase or decrease that the function models.

21. $y = 1700(0.75)^x$ **22.** $y = 30.698\left(\dfrac{5}{8}\right)^x$ **23.** $y = 984.5(1.73)^x$

24. The value of a piece of equipment has a decay factor of 0.80 per year. After 5 yr, the equipment is worth $98,304. What was the original value of the equipment?

Practice 8-2

Properties of Exponential Functions

Evaluate each expression to four decimal places.

1. e^2

2. $e^{-2.5}$

3. $e^{\frac{1}{3}}$

4. $e^{\sqrt{2}}$

Find the amount in a continuously compounded account for the given conditions.

5. principal: $5000
annual interest rate: 6.9%
time: 30 yr

6. principal: $20,000
annual interest rate: 3.75%
time: 2 yr

7. Hg-197 is used in kidney scans. It has a half-life of 64.128 h. Write the exponential decay function for a 12-mg sample. Find the amount remaining after 72 h.

8. Sr-85 is used in bone scans. It has a half-life of 64.9 days. Write the exponential decay function for an 8-mg sample. Find the amount remaining after 100 days.

9. I-123 is used in thyroid scans. It has a half-life of 13.2 h. Write the exponential decay function for a 45-mg sample. Find the amount remaining after 5 h.

Without graphing, determine whether each equation represents exponential growth or exponential decay.

10. $y = \frac{5}{4}(0.11)^x$

11. $A(t) = 1000(1.075)^t$

12. $s(t) = 2.4(0.5)^t$

13. Suppose you invest $5000 at an annual interest of 6.9%, compounded monthly.

   a. How much will you have in the account after 10 years?

   b. Determine how much more you would have if the interest were compounded continuously.

14. How long would it take to double your principal at an annual interest rate of 7% compounded continuously?

Graph each exponential function.

15. $y = 2^x$

16. $y = 2^{x+1}$

17. $y = -(2)^{x+1}$

18. $y = 5(0.12)^x$

19. $y = 5^x$

20. $y = -0.1(5)^x$

21. $y = 5^{-x}$

22. $y = -0.1(5)^{-x}$

23. $y = \left(\frac{1}{3}\right)^x$

24. $y = 5\left(\frac{1}{3}\right)^x$

25. $y = -5\left(\frac{1}{3}\right)^x$

26. $y = 2(2)^{x+2}$

Practice 8-3

Logarithmic Functions as Inverses

Write each equation in exponential form.

1. $\log_4 256 = 4$

2. $\log_7 1 = 0$

3. $\log_2 32 = 5$

4. $\log 10 = 1$

5. $\log_5 5 = 1$

6. $\log_8 \frac{1}{64} = -2$

7. $\log_9 59{,}049 = 5$

8. $\log_{17} 289 = 2$

9. $\log_{56} 1 = 0$

10. $\log_{12} \frac{1}{144} = -2$

11. $\log_2 \frac{1}{1024} = -10$

12. $\log_3 6561 = 8$

Write each equation in logarithmic form.

13. $9^2 = 81$

14. $25^2 = 625$

15. $8^3 = 512$

16. $13^2 = 169$

17. $2^9 = 512$

18. $4^5 = 1024$

19. $5^4 = 625$

20. $10^{-3} = 0.001$

21. $4^{-3} = \frac{1}{64}$

22. $5^{-2} = \frac{1}{25}$

23. $8^{-1} = \frac{1}{8}$

24. $11^0 = 1$

25. $6^1 = 6$

26. $6^{-3} = \frac{1}{216}$

27. $17^0 = 1$

28. $17^1 = 17$

29. A single-celled bacterium divides every hour. The number N of bacteria after t hours is given by the formula $\log_2 N = t$. After how many hours will there be 32 bacteria?

Evaluate each logarithm.

30. $\log_2 16$

31. $\log_2 8$

32. $\log_2 4$

33. $\log_2 2$

34. $\log_2 1$

35. $\log_2 \frac{1}{2}$

36. $\log_2 \frac{1}{4}$

37. $\log_2 \frac{1}{8}$

38. $\log_{16} 16$

39. $\log_5 125$

40. $\log_{11} 121$

41. $\log 0.1$

42. $\log 1$

43. $\log_3 1$

44. $\log_6 216$

45. $\log_{12} 12$

46. $\log_{30} 30$

47. $\log 100{,}000$

48. $\log_3 \frac{1}{9}$

49. $\log_3 \frac{1}{27}$

50. $\log \frac{1}{100}$

51. $\log_4 32$

52. $\log_7 \frac{1}{49}$

53. $\log_{81} 9$

For each pH given, find the concentration of hydrogen ions $[H^+]$. Use the formula $pH = -\log[H^+]$.

54. 7.2

55. 7.3

56. 8.2

57. 6.2

58. 5.6

59. 4.6

60. 7.0

61. 2.9

Graph each logarithmic function.

62. $y = \log x$

63. $y = \log_3 x$

64. $y = \log_6 x$

65. $y = \log_{\frac{1}{2}} x$

66. $y = \log_3(x + 1)$

67. $y = \log_2 x - 3$

68. $y = \log_6(x + 2)$

69. $y = \log_5(x - 4) + 1$

70. $y = \log_2(x - 3) + 1$

Practice 8-4

For Exercises 1–2, use the formula $L = 10 \log \frac{I}{I_0}$.

1. A sound has an intensity of $5.92 \times 10^{25} \text{W/m}^2$. What is the loudness of the sound in decibels? Use $I_0 = 10^{-12} \text{W/m}^2$.

2. Suppose you decrease the intensity of a sound by 45%. By how many decibels would the loudness be decreased?

Assume that $\log 3 \approx 0.4771$, $\log 4 \approx 0.6021$, and $\log 5 \approx 0.6990$. Use the properties of logarithms to evaluate each expression. Do not use a calculator.

3. $\log 12$ 4. $\log 16$ 5. $\log \frac{3}{5}$ 6. $\log 0.8$

7. $\log 75$ 8. $\log \frac{16}{5}$ 9. $\log_6 1 - \log 1$ 10. $\log 60$

Write each logarithmic expression as a single logarithm.

11. $\log_5 4 + \log_5 3$ 12. $\log_6 25 - \log_6 5$ 13. $\log_2 4 + \log_2 2 - \log_2 8$

14. $5 \log_7 x - 2 \log_7 x$ 15. $\log_4 60 - \log_4 4 + \log_4 x$ 16. $\log 7 - \log 3 + \log 6$

17. $2 \log x - 3 \log y$ 18. $\frac{1}{2} \log r + \frac{1}{3} \log s - \frac{1}{4} \log t$ 19. $\log_3 4x + 2 \log_3 5y$

20. $5 \log 2 - 2 \log 2$ 21. $\frac{1}{3} \log 3x + \frac{2}{3} \log 3x$ 22. $2 \log 4 + \log 2 + \log 2$

23. $(\log 3 - \log 4) - \log 2$ 24. $5 \log x + 3 \log x^2$ 25. $\log_6 3 - \log_6 6$

26. $\log 2 + \log 4 - \log 7$ 27. $\log_3 2x - 5 \log_3 y$ 28. $\frac{1}{3}(\log_2 x - \log_2 y)$

29. $\frac{1}{2} \log x + \frac{1}{3} \log y - 2 \log z$ 30. $3(4 \log t^2)$ 31. $\log_5 y - 4(\log_5 r + 2 \log_5 t)$

Expand each logarithm.

32. $\log xyz$ 33. $\log_2 \frac{x}{yz}$ 34. $\log 6x^3 y$

35. $\log 7(3x - 2)^2$ 36. $\log \sqrt{\frac{2rst}{5w}}$ 37. $\log \frac{5x}{4y}$

38. $\log_5 5x^{-5}$ 39. $\log \frac{2x^2 y}{3k^3}$ 40. $\log_4 (3xyz)^2$

State the property or properties used to rewrite each expression.

41. $\log 6 - \log 3 = \log 2$ 42. $6 \log 2 = \log 64$ 43. $\log 3x = \log 3 + \log x$

44. $\frac{1}{3} \log_2 x = \log_2 \sqrt[3]{x}$ 45. $\frac{2}{3} \log 7 = \log \sqrt[3]{49}$ 46. $\log_4 20 - 3 \log_4 x = \log_4 \frac{20}{x^3}$

Practice 8-5

Exponential and Logarithmic Equations

Use the Change of Base Formula to evaluate each expression. Round answers to the nearest hundredth.

1. $\log_2 12$ **2.** $\log_3 40$ **3.** $\log_4 8$ **4.** $\log_5 3$ **5.** $\log_2 1$

6. $\log_5 10$ **7.** $\log_2 8$ **8.** $\log_3 6$ **9.** $\log_9 3$ **10.** $\log_8 3$

Solve each equation. Check your answer. Round answers to the nearest hundredth.

11. $2^x = 243$ **12.** $7^n = 12$ **13.** $5^{2x} = 20$ **14.** $8^{n+1} = 3$

15. $4^{n-2} = 3$ **16.** $4^{3n} = 5$ **17.** $15^{2n-3} = 245$ **18.** $4^x - 5 = 12$

Solve each equation. Check your answer. Round answers to the nearest hundredth.

19. $\log 3x = 2$ **20.** $4 \log x = 4$ **21.** $\log (3x - 2) = 3$

22. $2 \log x - \log 5 = -2$ **23.** $\log 8 - \log 2x = -1$ **24.** $\log (x + 21) + \log x = 2$

25. $8 \log x = 16$ **26.** $\log x = 2$ **27.** $\log 4x = 2$

28. $\log (x - 25) = 2$ **29.** $2 \log x = 2$ **30.** $\log 3x - \log 5 = 1$

Use the Change of Base Formula to solve each equation. Round answers to the nearest hundredth.

31. $10^x = 182$ **32.** $8^n = 12$ **33.** $10^{2x} = 9$ **34.** $5^{n+1} = 3$

35. $10^{n-2} = 0.3$ **36.** $3^{3n} = 50$ **37.** $10^{2n-5} = 500$ **38.** $11^x - 50 = 12$

The function $y = 1000(1.005)^x$ models the value of $1000 deposit at 6% per year (0.005 per month) x months after the money is deposited.

39. Use a graph (on your graphing calculator) to predict how many months it will be until the account is worth $1100.

40. Predict how many years it will be until the account is worth $5000.

Solve each equation. Round answers to the nearest hundredth.

41. $2 \log 3x - \log 9 = 1$ **42.** $\log x - \log 4 = -1$ **43.** $\log x - \log 4 = -2$

44. $\log x - \log 4 = 3$ **45.** $2 \log x - \log 4 = 2$ **46.** $\log (2x + 5) = 3$

47. $2 \log (2x + 5) = 4$ **48.** $\log 4x = -1$ **49.** $2 \log x - \log 3 = 1$

Solve by graphing. Round answers to the nearest hundredth.

50. $10^n = 3$ **51.** $10^{3y} = 5$ **52.** $10^{k-2} = 20$

53. $5^x = 4$ **54.** $2^{4x} = 8$ **55.** $3^{x+5} = 15$

Practice 8-6

The formula $P = 50e^{-\frac{t}{25}}$ gives the power output P, in watts, available to run
a certain satellite for t days. Find how long a satellite with the given power
output will operate. Round answers to the nearest hundredth.

1. 10 W **2.** 12 W **3.** 14 W

The formula for the maximum velocity v of a rocket is $v = c \ln R$,
where c is the velocity of the exhaust in km/s and R is the mass ratio of the
rocket. A rocket must reach 7.8 km/s to attain a stable orbit. Round answers
to the nearest hundredth.

4. Find the maximum velocity of a rocket with a mass ratio of about
18 and an exhaust velocity of 2.2 km/s. Can this rocket achieve a
stable orbit?

5. What mass ratio would be needed to achieve a stable orbit for a rocket
with an exhaust velocity of 2.5 km/s?

6. A rocket with an exhaust velocity of 2.4 km/s can reach a maximum
velocity of 7.8 km/s. What is the mass ratio of the rocket?

Use natural logarithms to solve each equation. Round answers to the nearest
hundredth.

7. $e^x = 15$ **8.** $4e^x = 10$ **9.** $e^{x+2} = 50$ **10.** $4e^{3x-1} = 5$

11. $e^{x-4} = 2$ **12.** $5e^{6x+3} = 0.1$ **13.** $e^x = 1$ **14.** $e^{\frac{x}{5}} = 32$

15. $3e^{3x-5} = 49$ **16.** $7e^{5x+8} = 0.23$ **17.** $6 - e^{12x} = 5.2$ **18.** $e^{\frac{x}{2}} = 25$

19. $e^{2x} = 25$ **20.** $e^{\ln 5x} = 20$ **21.** $e^{\ln x} = 21$ **22.** $e^{x+6} + 5 = 1$

Solve each equation. Check your answer. Round answers to the nearest
hundredth.

23. $4 \ln x = -2$ **24.** $2 \ln (3x - 4) = 7$ **25.** $5 \ln (4x - 6) = -6$

26. $-7 + \ln 2x = 4$ **27.** $3 - 4 \ln (8x + 1) = 12$ **28.** $\ln x + \ln 3x = 14$

29. $2 \ln x + \ln x^2 = 3$ **30.** $\ln x + \ln 4 = 2$ **31.** $\ln x - \ln 5 = -1$

32. $\ln e^x = 3$ **33.** $3 \ln e^{2x} = 12$ **34.** $\ln e^{x+5} = 17$

35. $\ln 3x + \ln 2x = 3$ **36.** $5 \ln (3x - 2) = 15$ **37.** $7 \ln (2x + 5) = 8$

38. $\ln (3x + 4) = 5$ **39.** $\ln \frac{2x}{41} = 2$ **40.** $\ln (2x - 1)^2 = 4$

Write each expression as a single natural logarithm.

41. $\ln 16 - \ln 8$ **42.** $3 \ln 3 + \ln 9$ **43.** $a \ln 4 - \ln b$

44. $\ln z - 3 \ln x$ **45.** $\frac{1}{2} \ln 9 + \ln 3x$ **46.** $4 \ln x + 3 \ln y$

Practice 9-1

Each ordered pair is from an inverse variation. Find the constant of variation.

1. $\left(3, \frac{1}{3}\right)$ **2.** $(0.2, 6)$ **3.** $(10, 5)$ **4.** $\left(\frac{5}{7}, \frac{2}{5}\right)$ **5.** $(3.5, 1.2)$

Suppose that x and y vary inversely. Write a function that models each inverse variation.

6. $x = 7$ when $y = 2$

7. $x = 4$ when $y = 9$

8. $x = -3$ when $y = 8$

9. $x = 5$ when $y = -6$

10. $x = 1$ when $y = 0.8$

11. $x = -4$ when $y = -2$

12. $x = \frac{3}{5}$ when $y = 5$

13. $x = 3$ when $y = 2.1$

14. $x = -\frac{1}{3}$ when $y = \frac{9}{10}$

Describe the combined variation that is modeled by each formula.

15. $I = \frac{120}{R}$ **16.** $A = \frac{1}{2}bh$ **17.** $h = \frac{3V}{B}$ **18.** $V = \frac{4}{3}\pi r^3$

Each pair of values is from an inverse variation. Find the missing value.

19. $(2, 4)$ and $(6, y)$ **20.** $\left(\frac{1}{3}, 6\right)$ and $\left(x, -\frac{1}{2}\right)$ **21.** $(1.2, 4.5)$ and $(2.7, y)$

Suppose that x and y vary inversely. Write a function that models each inverse variation, and find y when $x = 8$.

22. $x = 4$ when $y = 2$ **23.** $x = -3$ when $y = \frac{1}{3}$ **24.** $x = 6$ when $y = 1.2$

Write the function that models each relationship. Find z when $x = 6$ and $y = 4$.

25. z varies jointly with x and y. When $x = 7$ and $y = 2$, $z = 28$.

26. z varies directly with x and inversely with the cube of y. When $x = 8$ and $y = 2$, $z = 3$.

Is the relationship between the values in each table a direct variation, an inverse variation, or neither? Write equations to model the direct and inverse variations.

27.

x	2	4	5	20
y	10	5	4	1

28.

x	1	3	7	10
y	2	8	20	29

29.

x	1	2	5	7
y	6	12	30	42

30.

x	0.2	0.5	2	3
y	25	62.5	250	375

31.

x	0.1	0.5	1.5	2
y	31	7	3	2.5

32.

x	3	1.5	0.5	0.3
y	5	10	30	50

Practice 9-2

Write an equation for a translation of $y = -\frac{3}{x}$ that has the given asymptotes.

1. $x = 2; y = 1$ **2.** $x = -1; y = 3$ **3.** $x = 4; y = -2$ **4.** $x = 0; y = 6$

5. $x = 3; y = 0$ **6.** $x = 1; y = 2$ **7.** $x = -3; y = -1$ **8.** $x = -2; y = 1$

Sketch the asymptotes and the graph of each equation.

9. $y = \frac{3}{x-1} + 2$ **10.** $y = \frac{2}{x+1}$ **11.** $y = \frac{11}{x+3} - 3$ **12.** $y = -\frac{4}{x-2} - 2$

13. $y = \frac{1}{x} + 3$ **14.** $y = \frac{1}{x+1} - 2$ **15.** $y = \frac{1}{x-2} + 1$ **16.** $y = \frac{1}{x-1} - 1$

17. $y = \frac{2}{x}$ **18.** $y = -\frac{3}{x-3} + 1$ **19.** $y = \frac{1}{x+1} + 2$ **20.** $y = \frac{3}{4x} + \frac{1}{2}$

21. $y = \frac{3}{x+3} - 1$ **22.** $y = \frac{2}{x-5}$ **23.** $y = -\frac{6}{x-3} - 2$ **24.** $y = \frac{5}{x}$

25. $y = \frac{1}{x-1} + 1$ **26.** $y = \frac{1}{x}$ **27.** $y = -\frac{3}{x-4} - 2$ **28.** $y = -\frac{1}{x-2} - \frac{1}{2}$

The length of a panpipe p (in feet) is inversely proportional to its pitch ℓ (in hertz). The inverse variation is modeled by the equation $p = \frac{495}{\ell}$.

29. Find the length required to produce a pitch of 220 Hz.

30. What pitch would be produced by a pipe with a length of 1.2 ft?

31. Find the pitch of a 0.6-ft pipe.

32. Find the pitch of a 3-ft pipe.

The junior class is buying keepsakes for the junior-senior prom. The price of each keepsake p is inversely proportional to the number of keepsakes s bought. The equation $p = \frac{1800}{s}$ models this inverse variation.

33. If they buy 240 keepsakes, how much can the class spend for each?

34. If they spend $5.55 for each keepsake, how many can the class buy?

35. If 400 keepsakes are bought, how much can be spent for each?

36. If the class buys 50 keepsakes, how much can be spent for each?

Compare the graphs of the inverse variations.

37. $y = \frac{1}{x}$ and $y = \frac{5}{x}$ **38.** $y = \frac{3}{x}$ and $y = -\frac{3}{x}$

39. $y = \frac{2}{x}$ and $y = \frac{20}{x}$ **40.** $y = -\frac{1}{x}$ and $y = -\frac{10}{x}$

41. $y = \frac{6}{x}$ and $y = -\frac{6}{x}$ **42.** $y = \frac{0.2}{x}$ and $y = \frac{0.02}{x}$

Practice 9-3

Find any points of discontinuity for each rational function.

1. $y = \dfrac{x + 3}{(x - 4)(x + 3)}$

2. $y = \dfrac{x - 2}{x^2 - 4}$

3. $y = \dfrac{(x - 3)(x + 1)}{(x - 2)}$

4. $y = \dfrac{3x(x + 2)}{x(x + 2)}$

5. $y = \dfrac{2}{(x + 1)}$

6. $y = \dfrac{4x}{x^3 - 9x}$

Find the horizontal asymptote of the graph of each rational function.

7. $y = \dfrac{2}{x - 6}$

8. $y = \dfrac{x + 2}{x - 4}$

9. $y = \dfrac{(x + 3)}{2(x + 4)}$

10. $y = \dfrac{2x^2 + 3}{x^2 - 6}$

11. $y = \dfrac{3x - 12}{x^2 - 2}$

12. $y = \dfrac{3x^3 - 4x + 2}{2x^3 + 3}$

Sketch the graph of each rational function.

13. $y = \dfrac{3}{x - 2}$

14. $y = \dfrac{3}{(x - 2)(x + 2)}$

15. $y = \dfrac{x}{x(x - 6)}$

16. $y = \dfrac{2x}{x - 6}$

17. $y = \dfrac{x^2 - 1}{x^2 - 4}$

18. $y = \dfrac{2x^2 + 10x + 12}{x^2 - 9}$

19. $y = \dfrac{x}{x^2 + 4}$

20. $y = \dfrac{x + 2}{x - 1}$

21. $y = \dfrac{x + 3}{x + 1}$

Describe the vertical asymptotes and holes for the graph of each rational function.

22. $y = \dfrac{x - 2}{(x + 2)(x - 2)}$

23. $y = -\dfrac{x}{x(x - 1)}$

24. $y = \dfrac{5 - x}{x^2 - 1}$

25. $y = \dfrac{x^2 - 2}{x + 2}$

26. $y = \dfrac{x^2 - 4}{x^2 + 4}$

27. $y = \dfrac{x + 3}{x^2 - 9}$

28. $y = \dfrac{x^2 - 25}{x - 4}$

29. $y = \dfrac{(x - 2)(2x + 3)}{(5x + 4)(x - 3)}$

30. $y = \dfrac{15x^2 - 7x - 2}{x^2 - 4}$

31. Suppose you start a home business typing technical research papers for college students. You must spend $3500 to replace your computer system. Then you estimate the cost of typing each page will be $.02.

    a. Write a rational function modeling your average cost per page. Graph the function.

    b. How many pages must you type to bring your average cost per page to less than $1.50 per page, the amount you plan to charge?

    c. How many pages must you type to have the average cost per page equal $1.00?

    d. How many pages must you type to have the average cost per page equal $.50?

    e. What are the vertical and horizontal asymptotes of the graph of the function?

Practice 9-4

Rational Expressions

Simplify each rational expression. State any restrictions on the variable.

1. $\dfrac{20 + 40x}{20x}$

2. $\dfrac{4x + 6}{2x + 3}$

3. $\dfrac{3y^2 - 3}{y^2 - 1}$

4. $\dfrac{4x + 20}{3x + 15}$

5. $\dfrac{x^2 + x}{x^2 + 2x}$

6. $\dfrac{3x + 6}{5x + 10}$

7. $\dfrac{2y}{y^2 + 6y}$

8. $\dfrac{x^2 - 5x}{x^2 - 25}$

9. $\dfrac{x^2 + 3x - 18}{x^2 - 36}$

10. $\dfrac{x^2 + 13x + 40}{x^2 - 2x - 35}$

11. $\dfrac{3x^2 - 12}{x^2 - x - 6}$

12. $\dfrac{4x^2 - 36}{x^2 + 10x + 21}$

13. $\dfrac{2x^2 + 11x + 5}{3x^2 + 17x + 10}$

14. $\dfrac{6x^2 + 5x - 6}{3x^2 - 5x + 2}$

15. $\dfrac{7x - 28}{x^2 - 16}$

16. $\dfrac{x^2 - 9}{2x + 6}$

Multiply or divide. Write the answer in simplest form. State any restrictions on the variables.

17. $\dfrac{5a}{5a + 5} \cdot \dfrac{10a + 10}{a}$

18. $\dfrac{9 - x^2}{5x^3 + 17x^2 + 6x} \cdot \dfrac{5x^2 + 2x}{x - 3}$

19. $\dfrac{(x - 1)(2x - 4)}{x + 4} \cdot \dfrac{(x + 1)(x + 4)}{2x - 4}$

20. $\dfrac{(x + 3)(x + 4)}{(x + 1)(x + 3)} \cdot \dfrac{(x + 3)(x + 1)}{x + 4}$

21. $\dfrac{5y - 20}{3y + 15} \cdot \dfrac{7y + 35}{10y + 40}$

22. $\dfrac{3x^3}{x^2 - 25} \cdot \dfrac{x^2 + 6x + 5}{x^2}$

23. $\dfrac{3y + 3}{6y + 12} \div \dfrac{18}{5y + 5}$

24. $\dfrac{6x + 6}{7} \div \dfrac{4x + 4}{x - 2}$

25. $\dfrac{y^2 - 2y}{y^2 + 7y - 18} \cdot \dfrac{y^2 - 81}{y^2 - 11y + 18}$

26. $\dfrac{(y + 6)^2}{y^2 - 36} \cdot \dfrac{3y - 18}{2y + 12}$

27. $\dfrac{y^2 - 49}{(y - 7)^2} \div \dfrac{5y + 35}{y^2 - 7y}$

28. $\dfrac{x^2 - 3x - 10}{2x^2 - 11x + 5} \div \dfrac{x^2 - 5x + 6}{2x^2 - 7x + 3}$

29. $\dfrac{x^2 - 5x + 4}{x^2 - 1} \cdot \dfrac{x^2 + 5x + 4}{x^2 - 9}$

30. $\dfrac{x^2 - 5x}{x^2 + 3x} \cdot \dfrac{x + 3}{x - 5}$

31. $\dfrac{x^2 - 4}{x^2 + 6x + 9} \cdot \dfrac{x^2 - 9}{x^2 + 4x + 4}$

32. $\dfrac{x^2 - 6x}{x^2 - 36} \cdot \dfrac{x + 6}{x^2}$

33. $\dfrac{x^2 + 10x + 16}{x^2 - 6x - 16} \div \dfrac{x + 8}{x^2 - 64}$

34. $\dfrac{5y}{2x^2} \div \dfrac{5y^2}{8x^2}$

35. $\dfrac{6x^2 - 32x + 10}{3x^2 - 15x} \div \dfrac{3x^2 + 11x - 4}{2x^2 - 32}$

36. $\dfrac{7x^4}{24y^5} \div \dfrac{21x}{12y^4}$

37. $\dfrac{2x + 4}{10x} \cdot \dfrac{15x^2}{x + 2}$

38. $\dfrac{x^2 + 6x}{3x^2 + 6x - 24} \cdot \dfrac{x^2 + 2x - 8}{x + 6}$

39. $\dfrac{x^2 - 5x + 4}{x^2 + 3x - 28} \cdot \dfrac{x^2 + 2x - 3}{x^2 + 10x + 21}$

40. $\dfrac{x^2 + 2x + 1}{x^2 - 1} \cdot \dfrac{x^2 + 3x + 2}{x^2 + 4x + 4}$

Practice 9-5

Adding and Subtracting Rational Expressions

Find the least common multiple of each pair of polynomials.

1. $3x(x + 2)$ and $6x(2x - 3)$

2. $2x^2 - 8x + 8$ and $3x^2 + 27x - 30$

3. $4x^2 + 12x + 9$ and $4x^2 - 9$

4. $2x^2 - 18$ and $5x^3 + 30x^2 + 45x$

Simplify.

5. $\dfrac{x^2}{5} + \dfrac{x^2}{5}$

6. $\dfrac{x^2 - 2}{12} + \dfrac{x}{6}$

7. $\dfrac{12}{xy^3} - \dfrac{9}{xy^3}$

8. $-\dfrac{2}{n + 4} - \dfrac{n^2}{n^2 - 16}$

9. $\dfrac{x}{9} - \dfrac{2x}{9}$

10. $\dfrac{2y + 1}{3y} + \dfrac{5y + 4}{3y}$

11. $\dfrac{6y - 4}{y^2 - 5} + \dfrac{3y + 1}{y^2 - 5}$

12. $\dfrac{6}{5x^2y} + \dfrac{5}{10xy^2}$

13. $\dfrac{3}{8x^3y^3} - \dfrac{1}{4xy}$

14. $\dfrac{4}{x^2 - 25} + \dfrac{6}{x^2 + 6x + 5}$

15. $\dfrac{3}{7x^2y} + \dfrac{4}{21xy^2}$

16. $\dfrac{xy - y}{x - 2} - \dfrac{y}{x + 2}$

17. $\dfrac{x + 2}{x^2 + 4x + 4} + \dfrac{2}{x + 2}$

18. $\dfrac{3}{x^2 - x - 6} + \dfrac{2}{x^2 + 6x + 5}$

19. $\dfrac{1}{6x^2 - 11x + 3} + \dfrac{1}{8x^2 - 18}$

20. $\dfrac{4}{x^2 - 3x} + \dfrac{6}{3x - 9}$

21. $\dfrac{3}{x^2 + 3x - 10} + \dfrac{1}{x^2 + 6x + 5}$

22. $\dfrac{3}{x - 9} + 4x$

23. $3 - \dfrac{1}{x^2 + 5}$

24. $5 + \dfrac{1}{x^2 - 5x + 6}$

25. $1 + \dfrac{2x + 7}{3x - 1}$

26. $\dfrac{2a}{a + 2} + \dfrac{3a}{a - 2}$

27. $\dfrac{4c}{c - 3} + \dfrac{4c}{c + 3}$

28. $\dfrac{f + 1}{fgh} + \dfrac{f - 1}{fgh}$

29. $\dfrac{2 - t}{t - 5} + \dfrac{2 + t}{t + 5}$

30. $\dfrac{4r}{r - 2} + \dfrac{4r}{r + 2}$

31. $\dfrac{x - y}{x + y} + \dfrac{y}{x}$

32. $\dfrac{\frac{2}{x}}{\frac{3}{y}}$

33. $\dfrac{1 + \frac{2}{x}}{4 - \frac{6}{x}}$

34. $\dfrac{\frac{1}{x - 2}}{2 + \frac{1}{x}}$

35. $\dfrac{y}{4y + 8} - \dfrac{1}{y^2 + 2y}$

36. $\dfrac{1 + \frac{2}{3}}{\frac{4}{9}}$

37. $\dfrac{6x^2}{3x - 2} + \dfrac{5x - 6}{3x - 2}$

38. $\dfrac{\frac{3}{x + 1}}{\frac{5}{x - 1}}$

39. $\dfrac{\frac{2}{x} + 6}{\frac{1}{y}}$

40. $\dfrac{2y}{y^2 - 4y - 12} + \dfrac{y}{y^2 - 10y + 24}$

41. The total resistance for a parallel circuit is given by

$\dfrac{1}{R} = \dfrac{1}{R_1} + \dfrac{1}{R_2} + \dfrac{1}{R_3}$.

   a. If $R = 1$ ohm, $R_2 = 6$ ohms, and $R_3 = 8$ ohms, find R_1.

   b. If $R_1 = 3$ ohms, $R_2 = 4$ ohms, and $R_3 = 6$ ohms, find R.

Practice 9-6

Solving Rational Equations

Solve each equation. Check each solution.

1. $\frac{1}{x} = \frac{x}{9}$

2. $\frac{4}{x} = \frac{x}{4}$

3. $\frac{3x}{4} = \frac{5x+1}{3}$

4. $-\frac{4}{x+1} = \frac{5}{3x+1}$

5. $\frac{3}{2x-3} = \frac{1}{5-2x}$

6. $\frac{x-4}{3} = \frac{x-2}{2}$

7. $\frac{3}{1-x} = \frac{2}{1+x}$

8. $\frac{2x-3}{4} = \frac{2x-5}{6}$

9. $\frac{1}{x} = \frac{2}{x+3}$

10. $\frac{x-1}{6} = \frac{x}{4}$

11. $\frac{3-x}{6} = \frac{6-x}{12}$

12. $\frac{4}{x+3} = \frac{10}{2x-1}$

13. $\frac{x-2}{10} = \frac{x-7}{5}$

14. $\frac{3}{3-x} = \frac{4}{2-x}$

15. $\frac{1}{4-5x} = \frac{3}{x+9}$

16. $x + \frac{10}{x-2} = \frac{x^2+3x}{x-2}$

17. $\frac{2}{x+3} + \frac{5}{3-x} = \frac{6}{x^2-9}$

18. $\frac{1}{2x+2} + \frac{5}{x^2-1} = \frac{1}{x-1}$

19. $\frac{2}{6x+2} = \frac{x}{3x^2+11}$

20. $\frac{3}{2x-4} = \frac{5}{3x+7}$

21. $\frac{2y}{5} + \frac{2}{6} = \frac{y}{2} - \frac{1}{6}$

22. $\frac{1}{2x+2} = \frac{1}{x-1}$

23. $\frac{2}{x+2} + \frac{5}{x-2} = \frac{6}{x^2-4}$

24. $5 + \frac{5}{x} = \frac{6}{5x}$

25. $\frac{4}{x-1} = \frac{5}{x-2}$

26. $\frac{2x-1}{x+3} = \frac{5}{3}$

27. $\frac{7}{2} = \frac{7x}{8} - 4$

28. $5 - \frac{4}{x+1} = 6$

29. $\frac{x}{x+3} - \frac{x}{x-3} = \frac{x^2+9}{x^2-9}$

30. $\frac{x}{3} + \frac{x}{2} = 10$

31. $\frac{2}{3} + \frac{3x-1}{6} = \frac{5}{2}$

32. $4 + \frac{2y}{y-5} = \frac{8}{y-5}$

33. $\frac{4}{x-3} = \frac{2}{x+1} + \frac{16}{x^2-2x-3}$

34. $\frac{7}{x^2-5x} + \frac{2}{x} = \frac{3}{2x-10}$

35. $\frac{x+3}{x^2+3x-4} = \frac{x+2}{x^2-16}$

36. $\frac{3y}{5} + \frac{1}{2} = \frac{y}{10}$

37. A round trip flight took 3.9 h flying time. The plane traveled the 510 mi to the city at 255 mi/h with no wind. How strong was the wind on the return flight? Was the wind a head wind or a tail wind?

38. A round trip flight took 5 h flying time. The plane traveled the 720 mi to the city at 295 mi/h with no wind. How strong was the wind on the return flight? Was the wind a head wind or a tail wind?

39. If one student can complete the decorations for the prom in 5 days working alone, another student could do it in 3 days, and a third could do it in 4 days, how long would it take them working together?

40. Tom and Huck start a business painting fences. They paint Aunt Polly's fence and find that they can paint a 200-ft^2 fence in 40 min if they work together. If Huck works four times faster than Tom, how long would it take each of them to paint a 500-ft^2 fence working alone?

Practice 9-7

Integers from 1 to 100 are randomly selected. State whether the events are mutually exclusive.

1. Even integers and multiples of 3

2. Integers less than 40 and integers greater than 50

3. Odd integers and multiples of 4

4. Integers less than 50 and integers greater than 40

Classify each pair of events as *dependent* or *independent*.

5. A member of the junior class and a second member of the same class are randomly selected.

6. A member of the junior class and a member of another class are randomly chosen.

7. An odd-numbered problem is assigned for homework, and an even-numbered problem is picked for a test.

8. The sum and the product of two rolls of a number cube

Find each probability.

9. A flavored-water company wants to know how many people prefer its new lemon-flavored water over two competitors' brands. The company hires you to survey 1000 people and ask them to rank the three drinks in order of preference. After conducting the survey, you find that 35% prefer the lemon-flavored water over Competitor A, 38% prefer the lemon-flavored water over Competitor B, and 47% did not prefer the lemon-flavored water over either competitor's brand. What is the probability that someone prefers the lemon-flavored water over both competitors' brands?

10. A natural number from 1 to 10 is randomly chosen.

   a. P(even or 7)

   b. P(even or odd)

   c. P(multiple of 2 or multiple of 3)

   d. P(odd or less than 3)

11. A standard number cube is tossed.

   a. P(even or 3)

   b. P(less than 2 or even)

   c. P(prime or 4)

   d. P(2 or greater than 6)

12. Only 93% of the airplane parts Salome is examining pass inspection. What is the probability that all of the next five parts pass inspection?

13. There is a 50% chance of thunderstorms the next three days. What is the probability that there will be thunderstorms each of the next three days?

Q and R are independent events. Find $P(Q$ and $R)$.

14. $P(Q) = \frac{1}{8}, P(R) = \frac{2}{5}$

15. $P(Q) = 0.8, P(R) = 0.2$

16. $P(Q) = \frac{1}{4}, P(R) = \frac{1}{5}$

M and N are mutually exclusive events. Find $P(M$ or $N)$.

17. $P(M) = \frac{3}{4}, P(N) = \frac{1}{6}$

18. $P(M) = 10\%, P(N) = 45\%$

19. $P(M) = \frac{1}{5}, P(N) = 18\%$

Practice 10-1

Identify the center and intercepts of each conic section. Give the domain and range of each graph.

1.

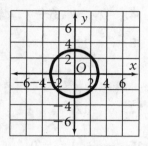

2.

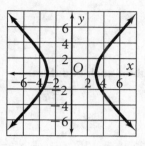

3.

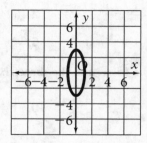

4.

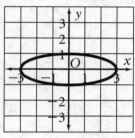

5.

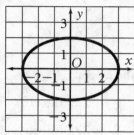

6.

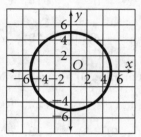

Graph each equation. Identify the conic section and its lines of symmetry. Then find the domain and range.

7. $x^2 + 4y^2 = 4$

8. $4x^2 + y^2 - 4 = 0$

9. $9x^2 + 4y^2 = 36$

10. $x^2 - y^2 = 4$

11. $x^2 - y^2 - 9 = 0$

12. $4x^2 - 9y^2 - 36 = 0$

13. $5x^2 + 5y^2 = 45$

14. $2x^2 + 2y^2 - 4 = 0$

15. $8x^2 + 8y^2 = 40$

16. $3x^2 + 6y^2 - 6 = 0$

17. $3x^2 - 6y^2 = 6$

18. $6y^2 - 3x^2 - 6 = 0$

19. $5x^2 - 5y^2 = 25$

20. $5x^2 + 5y^2 = 125$

21. $9x^2 + 16y^2 = 144$

22. $16y^2 - 9x^2 = 144$

23. $9x^2 - 16y^2 = 144$

24. $9x^2 + 9y^2 = 1$

25. $x^2 - y^2 = 49$

26. $2x^2 + 2y^2 - 32 = 0$

27. $2x^2 + 8y^2 = 32$

28. $y^2 - x^2 + 4 = 0$

29. $49x^2 - y^2 - 48 = 1$

30. $x^2 + y^2 - 40 = 9$

31. $5x^2 - 5y^2 - 45 = 0$

32. $25x^2 + y^2 = 25$

33. $9x^2 + 36y^2 = 36$

34. $25x^2 - y^2 - 25 = 0$

35. $y^2 - x^2 = 9$

36. $4y^2 - 9x^2 = 36$

37. $x^2 + y^2 = 4$

38. $x^2 + y^2 = 36$

39. $3x^2 + 3y^2 - 9 = 0$

40. $4x^2 + 9y^2 - 36 = 0$

41. $6x^2 + y^2 - 12 = 0$

42. $9x^2 + y^2 = 9$

Practice 10-2

Parabolas

Determine whether each parabola opens upward, downward, to the left, or to the right.

1. $x = -2y^2$ **2.** $y = -6x^2$ **3.** $-8x = y^2$ **4.** $-2y = -3x^2$

5. $-2y + x^2 = 0$ **6.** $2x + 6y^2 = 0$ **7.** $-3x + 4y^2 = 0$ **8.** $y + 12x^2 = 0$

Identify the focus and the directrix of the graph of each equation.

9. $y = -\frac{1}{32}x^2$ **10.** $y = -8x^2$ **11.** $x = \frac{1}{3}y^2$ **12.** $x = 12y^2$

13. $y + 3x^2 = 0$ **14.** $x - 5y^2 = 0$ **15.** $-y + x^2 = 3$ **16.** $-x - 3y^2 = 0$

17. $8x = y^2 + 6y + 9$ **18.** $\frac{1}{8}x = y^2$ **19.** $-8y = -x^2$ **20.** $-\frac{1}{8}y = -x^2$

Write an equation of a parabola with vertex at the origin.

21. focus at $(-2, 0)$ **22.** focus at $(0, 4)$ **23.** directrix at $x = 3$ **24.** directrix at $y = 4$

25. focus at $(0, -3)$ **26.** directrix at $x = -2$ **27.** directrix at $y = -3$ **28.** focus at $(3, 0)$

29. directrix at $x = 6$ **30.** focus at $(-5, 0)$ **31.** focus at $(0, 5)$ **32.** directrix at $y = -7$

Write the equation whose graph is the set of all points in the plane equidistant from the given point and the given line.

33. $F(0, 8)$ and $y = -8$ **34.** $F(1, 0)$ and $x = -1$ **35.** $F(6, 0)$ and $x = -6$

36. $F(0, -4)$ and $y = 4$ **37.** $F(0, 1)$ and $y = -1$ **38.** $F(-3, 0)$ and $x = 3$

39. $F(-1, 0)$ and $x = 1$ **40.** $F(-10, 0)$ and $x = 10$ **41.** $F(0, -3)$ and $y = 3$

42. $F(5, 0)$ and $x = -5$ **43.** $F(0, 5)$ and $y = -5$ **44.** $F(3, 0)$ and $x = -3$

45. A pipe with a diameter of 0.5 in. is located 10 in. from a mirror used as a parabolic solar collector. The pipe is at the focus of the parabola.

   a. Write an equation to model the cross section of the mirror.

   b. The pipe receives 25 times more sunlight than it would without the mirror. The amount of light collected by the mirror is directly proportional to its diameter. Find the width of the mirror.

Write an equation of a parabola opening upward with a vertex at the origin.

46. focus 2 units from vertex   **47.** focus $\frac{1}{4}$ unit from vertex

Identify the vertex, focus, and directrix of the graph of each equation. Then sketch the graph.

48. $y + 1 = -\frac{1}{4}(x - 3)^2$ **49.** $x = 2y^2$ **50.** $y^2 - 4x - 2y = 3$

Practice 10-3

Circles

Write an equation in standard form for each circle.

1.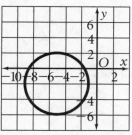

2.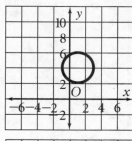

3.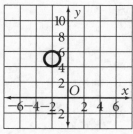

4.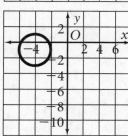

5.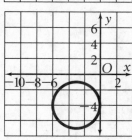

6.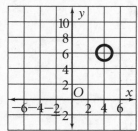

Write an equation of a circle with the given center and radius. Check your answers.

7. center $(0, 0)$, radius 3

8. center $(0, 1)$, radius 2

9. center $(-1, 0)$, radius 6

10. center $(2, 0)$, radius 1

11. center $(0, -3)$, radius 5

12. center $(4, -4)$, radius 1.5

13. center $(-2, 6)$, radius 4

14. center $(5, -1)$, radius 1.1

15. center $(1, -5)$, radius 2.5

16. center $(2, 3)$, diameter 1

Write an equation for each translation.

17. $x^2 + y^2 = 9$; right 4 and down 2

18. $x^2 + y^2 = 12$; left 2 and up 5

19. $x^2 + y^2 = 49$; right 1 and up 7

20. $x^2 + y^2 = 1$; right 5 and up 5

21. $x^2 + y^2 = 25$; up 10

22. $x^2 + y^2 = 36$; left 8 and down 6

Find the center and radius of each circle.

23. $(x + 1)^2 + (y - 8)^2 = 1$

24. $x^2 + (y + 3)^2 = 9$

25. $(x + 3)^2 + (y + 1)^2 = 2$

26. $(x - 6)^2 + y^2 = 5$

27. $(x - 6)^2 + (y - 9)^2 = 4$

28. $x^2 + y^2 = 144$

Use the center and radius to graph each circle.

29. $(x + 9)^2 + (y - 2)^2 = 81$

30. $x^2 + (y + 3)^2 = 121$

31. $(x - 8)^2 + (y + 9)^2 = 64$

32. $(x + 8)^2 + y^2 = 49$

33. $(x - 6)^2 + (y - 3)^2 = 75$

34. $(x + 9)^2 + (y + 9)^2 = 36$

35. $(x + 7)^2 + (y + 2)^2 = 80$

36. $(x - 5)^2 + (y + 7)^2 = 25$

Practice 10-4

Ellipses

● ●

Find the foci for each equation of an ellipse. Then graph the ellipse.

1. $\frac{x^2}{36} + \frac{y^2}{81} = 1$

2. $x^2 + \frac{y^2}{36} = 1$

3. $\frac{x^2}{9} + \frac{y^2}{100} = 1$

4. $16x^2 + 25y^2 = 1600$

5. $4x^2 + y^2 = 49$

6. $\frac{x^2}{64} + \frac{y^2}{144} = 1$

7. $9x^2 + 25y^2 = 225$

8. $25x^2 + 4y^2 = 100$

9. $\frac{x^2}{81} + \frac{y^2}{9} = 1$

10. $\frac{x^2}{121} + \frac{y^2}{4} = 1$

11. $49x^2 + y^2 = 49$

12. $4x^2 + 9y^2 = 36$

13. $\frac{x^2}{4} + \frac{y^2}{9} = 1$

14. $\frac{x^2}{9} + \frac{y^2}{4} = 1$

15. $\frac{x^2}{16} + y^2 = 1$

16. $\frac{x^2}{25} + \frac{y^2}{36} = 1$

17. $\frac{x^2}{81} + \frac{y^2}{16} = 1$

18. $x^2 + \frac{y^2}{25} = 1$

19. $3x^2 + 9y^2 = 9$

20. $4x^2 + 8y^2 = 16$

21. $12x^2 + 4y^2 = 48$

Write an equation of each ellipse in standard form with center at the origin and with the given characteristics.

22. height 8; width 18

23. vertices $(\pm 4, 0)$; co-vertices $(0, \pm 2)$

24. foci $(\pm 5, 0)$; co-vertices $(0, \pm 2)$

25. foci $(0, \pm 2)$; co-vertices $(\pm 1, 0)$

26. foci $(\pm 3, 0)$; co-vertices $(0, \pm 1)$

27. height 10; width 8

28. height 3; width 1

29. vertices $(\pm 2, 0)$; co-vertices $(0, \pm 1)$

30. foci $(\pm 1, 0)$; co-vertices $(0, \pm 2)$

31. foci $(0, \pm 3)$; co-vertices $(\pm 3, 0)$

32. vertex $(6, 0)$; co-vertex $(0, -5)$

33. vertex $(0, 10)$; co-vertex $(-7, 0)$

34. height 28 ft; width 20 ft

35. height 20 ft; width 28 ft

36. height 50 ft; width 40 ft

37. height 9 cm; width 12 cm

38. vertex $(0, 2)$; co-vertex $(-1, 0)$

39. vertex $(4, 0)$; co-vertex $(0, 2)$

40. foci $(0, \pm 4)$; co-vertices $(\pm 4, 0)$

41. foci $(\pm 4, 0)$; co-vertices (0 ± 2)

42. vertex $(9, 0)$; co-vertex $(0, -6)$

43. vertex $(11, 0)$; co-vertex $(0, -10)$

44. foci $(\pm 2, 0)$; co-vertices $(0, \pm 4)$

45. foci $(\pm 1, 0)$; co-vertices $(0, \pm 5)$

46. foci $(\pm 3, 0)$; co-vertices $(0, \pm 3)$

47. foci $(0, \pm 2)$; co-vertices $(\pm 1, 0)$

48. vertex $(-7, 0)$; co-vertex $(0, -5)$

49. vertex $(-2, 0)$; co-vertex $(0, -1)$

50. Blinn College is building a new track for cycling teams. The track is to be elliptical. The available land is 200 yd long and 100 yd wide. Find the equation of the ellipse.

Practice 10-5

Hyperbolas

Find the foci of each graph. Then draw the graph.

1. $\dfrac{x^2}{4} - \dfrac{y^2}{4} = 1$

2. $\dfrac{y^2}{9} - \dfrac{x^2}{25} = 1$

3. $\dfrac{x^2}{49} - \dfrac{y^2}{36} = 1$

4. $4y^2 - 36x^2 = 144$

5. $x^2 - 9y^2 = 9$

6. $16x^2 - y^2 = 64$

7. $9y^2 - 16x^2 = 144$

8. $4x^2 - 9y^2 = 36$

9. $121y^2 - 4x^2 = 121$

10. $\dfrac{y^2}{16} - \dfrac{x^2}{9} = 1$

11. $\dfrac{x^2}{64} - \dfrac{y^2}{9} = 1$

12. $\dfrac{y^2}{100} - \dfrac{x^2}{4} = 1$

13. $25y^2 - 4x^2 = 100$

14. $49y^2 - x^2 = 49$

15. $4x^2 - 100y^2 = 100$

16. $\dfrac{x^2}{25} - \dfrac{y^2}{4} = 1$

17. $y^2 - \dfrac{x^2}{9} = 1$

18. $\dfrac{y^2}{25} - \dfrac{x^2}{16} = 1$

19. $\dfrac{y^2}{4} - \dfrac{x^2}{9} = 1$

20. $x^2 - \dfrac{y^2}{16} = 1$

21. $\dfrac{x^2}{4} - \dfrac{y^2}{16} = 1$

22. $\dfrac{x^2}{36} - y^2 = 1$

23. $\dfrac{x^2}{64} - \dfrac{y^2}{16} = 1$

24. $y^2 - x^2 = 16$

25. $y^2 - 4x^2 = 16$

26. $4x^2 - 4y^2 = 100$

27. $25x^2 - 4y^2 = 100$

28. $16y^2 - 4x^2 = 80$

29. $9y^2 - 4x^2 = 36$

30. $4x^2 - 36y^2 = 36$

31. $x^2 - 25y^2 = 25$

32. $4x^2 - y^2 = 16$

33. $9y^2 - 16x^2 = 225$

34. $16y^2 - 9x^2 = 225$

35. $4x^2 - 9y^2 = 36$

36. $9x^2 - 4y^2 = 36$

37. $\dfrac{y^2}{9} - x^2 = 1$

38. $\dfrac{x^2}{9} - \dfrac{y^2}{16} = 1$

39. $\dfrac{y^2}{4} - \dfrac{x^2}{16} = 1$

40. $\dfrac{x^2}{25} - \dfrac{y^2}{16} = 1$

41. $y^2 - \dfrac{x^2}{16} = 1$

42. $\dfrac{x^2}{9} - \dfrac{y^2}{36} = 1$

43. $4y^2 - 25x^2 = 100$

44. $y^2 - 4x^2 = 16$

45. $16x^2 - y^2 = 64$

Find the equation of a hyperbola with the given a and c values. Assume that the transverse axis is horizontal.

46. $a = 432{,}356,\ c = 1{,}984{,}576$

47. $a = 176{,}398,\ c = 1{,}984{,}576$

48. $a = 7,\ c = 9$

49. $a = 292{,}954,\ c = 365{,}987$

50. $a = 5,\ c = 15$

51. $a = 7654,\ c = 8675$

52. $a = 67,\ c = 92$

53. $a = 75,\ c = 180$

54. $a = 8,\ c = 20$

55. $a = 6,\ c = 9$

56. $a = 6,\ c = 10$

57. $a = 6,\ c = 8$

58. $a = 1,\ c = 9$

59. $a = 3,\ c = 7$

60. $a = 8,\ c = 10$

61. $a = 9,\ c = 12$

Practice 10-6

Identify the conic section represented by each equation by writing the equation in standard form. For a parabola, give the vertex. For a circle, give its center and radius. For an ellipse or hyperbola, give its center and foci. Sketch the graph.

1. $3x^2 + 6x + 5y^2 - 20y - 13 = 0$ **2.** $x^2 - 9y^2 + 36y - 45 = 0$

3. $x^2 + 4y^2 + 8x - 48 = 0$ **4.** $x^2 + y^2 - 8x - 4y + 19 = 0$

5. $x^2 + y^2 + 6y - 27 = 0$ **6.** $x^2 - 10x - 4y^2 + 24y - 15 = 0$

7. $16x^2 - 96x - 9y^2 + 36y - 36 = 0$ **8.** $10x^2 + 10y^2 - 70 = 0$

9. $x^2 + 2x + y^2 + 14y - 31 = 0$ **10.** $25x^2 + 50x - 9y^2 - 18y - 209 = 0$

11. $4x^2 - 16x + 4y^2 - 16y - 4 = 0$ **12.** $x^2 + 4y^2 - 4x + 8y = 0$

13. $x^2 - 10x + y^2 + 4y - 7 = 0$ **14.** $x^2 + 2x + y^2 - 10y - 38 = 0$

15. $x^2 - 2x - y + 3 = 0$ **16.** $x^2 + 6x - y + 7 = 0$

17. $x^2 + 8x + y^2 + 2y + 1 = 0$ **18.** $x^2 - y^2 - 4 = 0$

19. $y^2 + 2y - x + 3 = 0$ **20.** $x^2 - 4x + 3 - y = 0$

Write an equation of a conic section with the given characteristics.

21. circle with center $(-4, 5)$, radius 6

22. hyperbola with center $(-4, 5)$, one vertex $(-4, 7)$, one focus $(-4, 8)$

23. Points on the hyperbola are 96 units closer to one focus than to the other. The foci are located at $(0, 0)$ and $(100, 0)$.

24. parabola with vertex $(1, -2)$, x-intercept 3, and opens to the right

25. ellipse with center $(0, 2)$, horizontal major axis of length 6, minor axis of length 4

26. ellipse with center $(-4, -5)$, endpoints of major and minor axes $(-4, -7), (-4, -3), (-1, -5), (-7, -5)$

27. circle with center $(-1, 2)$, diameter 12

28. parabola with vertex $(-1, 5)$, y-intercept 4, and opens downward

29. hyperbola with vertices $(0, 2)$ and $(4, 2)$, foci $(-1, 2)$ and $(5, 2)$

30. ellipse with center $(2, -5)$, one end of each axis $(2, -9)$ and $(-3, -5)$

31. Points on the hyperbola are 12 units closer to one focus than to the other. The foci are located at $(0, 0)$ and $(250, 0)$.

32. ellipse with center $(0, -2)$, vertical major axis of length 5, minor axis of length 3

Practice 11-1

Mathematical Patterns

Write a recursive formula for each sequence. Then find the next term.

1. $-14, -8, -2, 4, 10, \ldots$

2. $6, 5.7, 5.4, 5.1, 4.8, \ldots$

3. $1, -2, 4, -8, 16, \ldots$

4. $1, 3, 9, 27, \ldots$

5. $1, \frac{1}{2}, \frac{1}{4}, \frac{1}{8}, \frac{1}{16}, \ldots$

6. $\frac{2}{3}, 1, 1\frac{1}{3}, 1\frac{2}{3}, 2, \ldots$

7. $36, 39, 42, 45, 48, \ldots$

8. $36, 30, 24, 18, 12, \ldots$

9. $9.6, 4.8, 2.4, 1.2, 0.6, \ldots$

Write an explicit formula for each sequence. Then find a_{20}.

10. $7, 14, 21, 28, 35, \ldots$

11. $2, 8, 14, 20, 26, \ldots$

12. $5, 6, 7, 8, 9, \ldots$

13. $-1, 0, 1, 2, 3, \ldots$

14. $3, 5, 7, 9, 11, \ldots$

15. $0.8, 1.6, 2.4, 3.2, 4, \ldots$

16. $\frac{1}{4}, \frac{1}{2}, \frac{3}{4}, 1, \frac{5}{4}, \ldots$

17. $\frac{1}{2}, \frac{1}{4}, \frac{1}{6}, \frac{1}{8}, \frac{1}{10}, \ldots$

18. $\frac{2}{3}, 1\frac{2}{3}, 2\frac{2}{3}, 3\frac{2}{3}, 4\frac{2}{3}, \ldots$

Describe each pattern formed. Find the next three terms.

19. $1, 2, 4, 8, 16, \ldots$

20. $44, 39, 34, 29, 24, \ldots$

21. $0.7, 0.8, 0.9, 1.0, 1.1, \ldots$

22. $4, 11, 18, 25, 32, \ldots$

23. $1\frac{1}{4}, 2\frac{1}{2}, 5, 10, 20, \ldots$

24. $-6, -9, -12, -15, -18, \ldots$

Decide whether each formula is *explicit* or *recursive*. Then find the first five terms of each sequence.

25. $a_n = \frac{1}{3}n$

26. $a_n = n^2 - 6$

27. $a_1 = 5, a_n = 3a_{n-1} - 7$

28. $a_n = \frac{1}{2}(n - 1)$

29. $a_1 = 5, a_n = 3 - a_{n-1}$

30. $a_1 = -4, a_n = 2a_{n-1}$

31. The first figure of a fractal contains one segment. For each successive figure, six segments replace each segment.

   a. How many segments are in each of the first four figures of the sequence?

   b. Write a recursive formula for the sequence.

32. The sum of the measures of the exterior angles of any polygon is 360. All the angles have the same measure in a regular polygon.

   a. Find the measure of one exterior angle in a regular hexagon (six angles).

   b. Write an explicit formula for the measure of one exterior angle in a regular polygon with n angles.

   c. Why would this formula not be meaningful for $n = 1$ or $n = 2$?

Practice 11-2

Arithmetic Sequences

Find the 43rd term of each sequence.

1. $12, 14, 16, 18, \ldots$

2. $13.1, 3.1, -6.9, -16.9, \ldots$

3. $19.5, 19.9, 20.3, 20.7, \ldots$

4. $27, 24, 21, 18, \ldots$

5. $2, 13, 24, 35, \ldots$

6. $21, 15, 9, 3, \ldots$

7. $1.3, 1.4, 1.5, 1.6, \ldots$

8. $-2.1, -2.3, -2.5, -2.7, \ldots$

9. $45, 48, 51, 54, \ldots$

Is the given sequence arithmetic? If so, identify the common difference.

10. $2, 3, 5, 8, \ldots$

11. $0, -3, -6, -9, \ldots$

12. $0.9, 0.5, 0.1, -0.3, \ldots$

13. $3, 8, 13, 18, \ldots$

14. $14, -15, -44, -73, \ldots$

15. $3.2, 3.5, 3.8, 4.1, \ldots$

16. $-34, -28, -22, -16, \ldots$

17. $2.3, 2.5, 2.7, 2.9, \ldots$

18. $127, 140, 153, 166, \ldots$

Find the missing term of each arithmetic sequence.

19. $\ldots 23, \blacksquare, 49, \ldots$

20. $14, \blacksquare, 28, \ldots$

21. $\ldots 29, \blacksquare, 33, \ldots$

22. $\ldots 14, \blacksquare, 15, \ldots$

23. $\ldots -45, \blacksquare, -39, \ldots$

24. $\ldots -5, \blacksquare, -2, \ldots$

25. $-2, \blacksquare, 2, \ldots$

26. $\ldots -6, \blacksquare, 2, \ldots$

27. $-34, \blacksquare, 77, \ldots$

28. $\ldots -45, \blacksquare, -12, \ldots$

29. $-2, \blacksquare, 456, \ldots$

30. $\ldots 34, \blacksquare, 345, \ldots$

Find the arithmetic mean a_n of the given terms.

31. $a_{n-1} = 2, a_{n+1} = 7$

32. $a_{n-1} = 13.2, a_{n+1} = 15.8$

33. $a_{n-1} = 29, a_{n+1} = -11$

34. $a_{n-1} = \frac{2}{5}, a_{n+1} = \frac{4}{5}$

35. $a_{n-1} = 15, a_{n+1} = -17$

36. $a_{n-1} = -6, a_{n+1} = -7$

37. Each year, a volunteer organization expects to add 5 more people to the number of shut-ins for whom the group provides home maintenance services. This year, the organization provides the service for 32 people.

   a. Write a recursive formula for the number of people the organization expects to serve each year.

   b. Write the first five terms of the sequence.

   c. Write an explicit formula for the number of people the organization expects to serve each year.

   d. How many people would the organization expect to serve in the 20th year?

Practice 11-3

Find the missing term of each geometric sequence.

1. $4, \blacksquare, 16, \ldots$

2. $9, \blacksquare, 16, \ldots$

3. $2, \blacksquare, 8, \ldots$

4. $3, \blacksquare, 12, \ldots$

5. $2, \blacksquare, 50, \ldots$

6. $4, \blacksquare, 5.76, \ldots$

Is the given sequence geometric? If so, identify the common ratio and find the next two terms.

7. $3, 9, 27, 81, \ldots$

8. $4, 8, 16, 32, \ldots$

9. $4, 8, 12, 16, \ldots$

10. $4, -8, 16, -32, \ldots$

11. $1, 0.5, 0.25, 0.125, \ldots$

12. $100, 30, 9, 2.7, \ldots$

13. $-5, 0, 5, 10, \ldots$

14. $64, -32, 16, -8, \ldots$

15. $1, 4, 9, 16, \ldots$

Identify each sequence as *arithmetic, geometric,* or *neither.* Then find the next two terms.

16. $9, 3, 1, \frac{1}{3}, \ldots$

17. $1, 0, -2, -5, \ldots$

18. $2, -2, 2, -2, \ldots$

19. $-3, 2, 7, 12, \ldots$

20. $1, -2, -5, -8, \ldots$

21. $1, -2, 3, -4, \ldots$

Write the explicit formula for each sequence. Then generate the first five terms.

22. $a_1 = 3, r = -2$

23. $a_1 = 5, r = 3$

24. $a_1 = -1, r = 4$

25. $a_1 = -2, r = -3$

26. $a_1 = 32, r = -0.5$

27. $a_1 = 2187, r = \frac{1}{3}$

28. $a_1 = 9, r = 2$

29. $a_1 = -4, r = 4$

30. $a_1 = 0.1, r = -2$

31. When a pendulum swings freely, the length of its arc decreases geometrically. Find each missing arc length.

   a. 20th arc is 20 in.; 22nd arc is 18.5 in.

   b. 8th arc is 27 mm; 10th arc is 3 mm

32. The deer population in an area is increasing. This year, the population was 1.025 times last year's population of 2537.

   a. Assuming that the population increases at the same rate for the next few years, write an explicit formula for the sequence.

   b. Find the expected deer population for the fourth year of the sequence.

33. You enlarge a picture to 150% of its size several times. After the first increase, the picture is 1 in. wide.

   a. Write an explicit formula to model the size after each increase.

   b. How wide is the photo after the 2nd increase?

   c. How wide is the photo after the 3rd increase?

   d. How wide is the photo after the 12th increase?

Practice 11-4

**For each sum, find the number of terms, the first term, and the last term.
Then evaluate the series.**

1. $\displaystyle\sum_{n=1}^{4} (n-1)$

2. $\displaystyle\sum_{n=2}^{6} (2n-1)$

3. $\displaystyle\sum_{n=3}^{8} (n+25)$

4. $\displaystyle\sum_{n=2}^{5} (5n+3)$

5. $\displaystyle\sum_{n=1}^{4} (2n+0.5)$

6. $\displaystyle\sum_{n=1}^{6} (3-n)$

7. $\displaystyle\sum_{n=5}^{10} n$

8. $\displaystyle\sum_{n=1}^{4} (-n-3)$

9. $\displaystyle\sum_{n=3}^{6} (3n+2)$

Write the related series for each finite sequence. Then evaluate each series.

10. $1, 3, 5, \ldots, 15$

11. $5, 8, 11, \ldots, 26$

12. $4, 9, 14, 19, \ldots, 44$

13. $10, 25, 40, 55, 70, 85$

14. $17, 25, 33, 41, 49, 57, 65$

15. $125, 126, 127, \ldots, 131$

**Use summation notation to write each arithmetic series for the specified
number of terms.**

16. $1 + 3 + 5 + \ldots; n = 7$

17. $2.3 + 2.6 + 2.9 + \ldots; n = 5$

18. $4 + 8 + 12 + \ldots; n = 4$

19. $10 + 7 + 4 + \ldots; n = 6$

20. $3 + 7 + 11 + \ldots; n = 8$

21. $15 + 25 + 35 + \ldots; n = 7$

**Tell whether each list is a *series* or a *sequence*. Then tell whether it is
finite or *infinite*.**

22. $7, 12, 17, 22, 27$

23. $3 + 5 + 7 + 9 + \ldots$

24. $8, 8.2, 8.4, 8.6, 8.8, 9.0, \ldots$

25. $1 + 5 + 9 + 13 + 17$

26. $40, 20, 10, 5, 2.5, 1.25, \ldots$

27. $10 + 20 + 30 + 40 + 50$

Each sequence has six terms. Evaluate each related series.

28. $1, 0, -1, \ldots, -4$

29. $4, 5, 6, \ldots, 9$

30. $-7, -9, -11, \ldots, -17$

31. $-6, -7, -8, \ldots, -11$

32. $0, 0.3, 0.6, \ldots, 1.5$

33. $5, 7, 9, \ldots, 15$

34. An embroidery pattern calls for 5 stitches in the first row and for three
more stitches in each successive row. The 25th row, which is the last row,
has 77 stitches. Find the total number of stitches in the pattern.

35. A marching band formation consists of 6 rows. The first row has 9
musicians, the second has 11, the third has 13 and so on. How many
musicians are in the last row and how many musicians are there in all?

Practice 11-5

Decide whether each infinite geometric series *diverges* or *converges*. State whether each series has a sum.

1. $3 + \frac{3}{2} + \frac{3}{4} + \ldots$ 　　　　**2.** $4 + 2 + 1 + \ldots$ 　　　　**3.** $17 + 15.3 + 13.77 + \ldots$

4. $6 + 11.4 + 21.66 + \ldots$ 　　**5.** $-20 - 8 - 3.2 - \ldots$ 　　**6.** $50 + 70 + 98 + \ldots$

Evaluate each infinite series that has a sum.

7. $\sum_{n=1}^{\infty} 5\left(\frac{2}{3}\right)^{n-1}$ 　　**8.** $\sum_{n=1}^{\infty} (-2.1)^{n-1}$ 　　**9.** $\sum_{n=1}^{\infty} \left(-\frac{1}{2}\right)^{n-1}$ 　　**10.** $\sum_{n=1}^{\infty} 2\left(\frac{5}{3}\right)^{n-1}$

Evaluate each infinite geometric series.

11. $8 + 4 + 2 + 1 + \ldots$ 　　　　　　**12.** $1 + \frac{1}{3} + \frac{1}{9} + \frac{1}{27} + \ldots$

13. $120 + 96 + 76.8 + 61.44 + \ldots$ 　　**14.** $1000 + 750 + 562.5 + 421.875 + \ldots$

Determine whether each series is *arithmetic* or *geometric*. Then evaluate the series to the given term.

15. $2 + 5 + 8 + 11 + \ldots ; S_9$ 　　　　**16.** $\frac{1}{8} + \frac{1}{16} + \frac{1}{32} + \frac{1}{64} + \ldots ; S_8$

17. $-3 + 6 - 12 + 24 - \ldots ; S_{10}$ 　　**18.** $-2 + 2 + 6 + 10 + \ldots ; S_{12}$

Evaluate the series to the given term.

19. $40 + 20 + 10 + \ldots ; S_{10}$ 　　　　**20.** $4 + 12 + 36 + \ldots ; S_{15}$

21. $15 + 12 + 9.6 + \ldots ; S_{40}$ 　　　　**22.** $27 + 9 + 3 + \ldots ; S_{100}$

23. $0.2 + 0.02 + 0.002 + \ldots ; S_8$ 　　　**24.** $100 + 200 + 400 + \ldots ; S_6$

25. This month, Julia deposits $400 to save for a vacation. She plans to deposit 10% more each successive month for the next 11 months. How much will she have saved after the 12 deposits?

26. Suppose your business made a profit of $5500 the first year. If the profit increases 20% per year, find the total profit over the first 5 yr.

27. The end of a pendulum travels 50 cm on its first swing. Each swing after the first travels 99% as far as the preceding one. How far will the pendulum travel before it stops?

28. A seashell has chambers that are each 0.82 times the length of the next chamber. The outer chamber is 32 mm around. Find the total length of the shell's spiraled chambers.

29. The first year a toy manufacturer introduces a new toy, its sales total $495,000. The company expects its sales to drop 10% each succeeding year. Find the total expected sales in the first 6 yr. Find the total expected sales if the company offers the toy for sale for as long as anyone buys it.

Practice 11-6

Write and evaluate a sum to approximate the area under each curve for the domain $0 \le x \le 2$.
   a. **Use inscribed rectangles 0.5 unit wide.**
   b. **Use circumscribed rectangles 0.5 unit wide.**

1. $y = -x^2 + 4$

2. $f(x) = -2x^2 + 16$

3. $g(x) = -0.5x^2 + 2$

4. $f(x) = x^2 + 4$

5. $y = 2x^2 + 6$

6. $h(g) = 0.5x^2 + 2$

7. $y = -3x^2 + 15$

8. $f(x) = 3x^2 + 2$

9. $f(x) = 10 - x^2$

10. a. Graph the curve $y = 2x^2 + 1$.

 b. Use inscribed rectangles to approximate the area under the curve
 for the interval $0 \le x \le 2$ and rectangle width of 0.5 unit.

 c. Repeat part b using circumscribed rectangles.

 d. Find the mean of the areas you found in parts b and c. Of the three
 estimates, which best approximates the area for the interval?

Use your graphing calculator to find the area under each curve for the domain $-2 \le x \le 1$.

11. $y = -x^3 + 1$

12. $f(x) = -2x^3 + 3$

13. $f(x) = 2x^2 + 1$

14. $g(x) = 3x^2 + 1$

15. $y = -\frac{1}{4}x^2 + 1$

16. $f(x) = 4x^2 + 2$

17. $y = -x^2 + 4$

18. $f(x) = x^2 + 1$

19. $y = \sqrt{x + 3}$

Given each set of axes, what does the area under the curve represent?

20. y-axis: feet per second, x-axis: seconds

21. y-axis: computers produced per day, x-axis: days

22. y-axis: miles per hour, x-axis: hours

23. y-axis: gallons per minute, x-axis: minutes

24. y-axis: molecules per second, x-axis: seconds

25. y-axis: price per pound of apples, x-axis: pounds of apples

Graph each curve. Use inscribed rectangles to approximate the area under the curve for the interval and rectangle width given.

26. $y = \frac{1}{4}x^2, 2 \le x \le 4, 1$

27. $y = x^3 + 1, 0 \le x \le 2, 0.5$

Practice 12-1

Probability Distributions

1. Use the frequency table to find each probability.

   a. What is the probability that a person living alone is 45 or older?

   b. In a sample of 100 persons living alone, predict how many are age 35 and older.

   c. Find P(15 to 24 years of age)

   d. Find P(35 to 44 years of age)

   e. Find P(65 years and older)

Persons Living Alone in 1999 (in thousands)	
15 to 24 years of age	1,313
25 to 34 years of age	3,714
35 to 44 years of age	4,074
45 to 64 years of age	7,757
65 years and older	9,747

Source: *www.infoplease.com*

2. You roll two number cubes. Make a table to show the probability distribution for each sample space.

   a. {the sum of the cubes is 5 or less, the sum is greater than 5}

   b. {the sum of the cubes is prime, the sum is composite}

   c. {only one cube shows 2, both cubes show the same number, the cubes show different numbers and neither is a 2}

3. A survey of student pizza preferences showed that 43 students preferred cheese, 56 preferred sausage, 39 preferred pepperoni, 28 preferred supreme, 31 preferred another kind, and 19 did not like any type of pizza.

   a. Organize this data in a frequency table.

   b. Find the experimental probability for each outcome in the table. Round to the nearest tenth of a percent. What is the sum of the experimental probabilities? Explain.

   c. Graph the probability distribution for {pizza, no pizza}.

   d. Graph the probability distribution for {cheese, sausage or pepperoni, supreme or other, no pizza}.

   e. How are the probability distributions related?

4. Visitors to the game preserve see up to eight species of large mammals as they drive through. A survey shows that the number of species seen varies according to the distribution below.

   Probability Distribution for Number of Species Seen

s	0	1	2	3	4	5	6	7	8
P(s)	0.08	0.12	0.21	0.18	0.12	0.11	0.09	0.08	0.01

   a. Use random numbers to simulate the number of species seen in each of 20 visits to the preserve. What is the average per visit?

   b. You donate $5 to the preserve for upkeep of each species you see. On the basis of your simulation, how much would you donate in 20 visits?

Practice 12-2

1. The table contains information about the 1205 employees at one business. Find each probability. Round to the nearest tenth of a percent.

Education and Salary of Employees

	Under $20,000	$20,000 to $30,000	Over $30,000
Less than high school	69	36	2
High school	112	98	14
Some college	102	193	143
College degree	13	178	245

   a. P(employee has less than a high school education)

   b. P(employee earns under $20,000)

   c. P(employee earns over $30,000 and has less than a high school education)

   d. P(employee earns under $20,000 and has a college degree)

   e. given that the employee has only a high school education, the probability that the employee earns over $30,000

   f. given that the employee earns over $30,000, the probability that the employee has only a high school education or less

2. High school students in one school chose their favorite leisure activity. Find each probability. Round to the nearest tenth of a percent.

Favorite Leisure Activities

	Sports	Hiking	Reading	Phoning	Shopping	Other
Female	39	48	85	62	71	29
Male	67	58	76	54	68	39

   a. P(sports | female)   **b.** P(female | sports)   **c.** P(reading | male)   **d.** P(male | reading)

   e. P(hiking | female)   **f.** P(hiking | male)   **g.** P(male | shopping)   **h.** P(female | shopping)

3. The senior class is 55% female, and 32% are females who play a competitive sport. Find the probability that a student plays a competitive sport, given that the student is female.

Draw a tree diagram. Find each probability.

4. A softball game has an 80% chance of being canceled for a light drizzle and a 30% chance of being canceled for a heavy fog when there is no drizzle. There is a 70% chance of heavy fog and a 30% chance of light drizzle.

   a. Find the probability that the game will be canceled.

   b. Find the probability there will be a light drizzle and the game will not be canceled.

5. The students of a high school are 51% males; 45% of the males and 49% of the females attend concerts.

   a. Find the probability that a student attends concerts.

   b. Find the probability that a student is a female and does not attend concerts.

Practice 12-3

Analyzing Data

Identify the outliers of each set of values.

1. 23 76 79 76 77 74 75

2. 43 46 49 50 52 54 78 47

3. 32 35 3 36 37 35 38 40 42 34

4. 153 156 176 156 165 110 159 169 172

Find the mean, median, and mode of each set of values.

5. 98 87 79 82 101 99 97 97 102 91 93

6. 41 41 45 46 54 52 53 50 49 47 49 48 44

7. 2.3 2.4 2.5 2.8 2.4 2.4 2.9 2.6 2.4 2.9

8. 15.2 15.3 15.9 16.1 16.3 15.4 15.5 15.6 15.8

9. 245 345 365 566 442 476 423 495 412

10. 1002 1005 1023 1034 1012 1054 1023

11. 0.019 0.021 0.018 0.019 0.018 0.020

12. 23 29 31 32 29 27 21 19 25 26 28 29 24

13. 45 49 41 45 51 39 42 46 49 48 42 40

14. 3 5 31 35 41 49 50 51 52 53 54 69 81 99

15. 14 15 19 15 15 16 19 20 21 29 16 17

16. 1.8 1.3 1.9 1.5 1.6 1.5 1.8 1.5 1.3 1.4 1.3

17. 8.7 8.8 8.9 9.4 10.2 9.8 9.0 8.1 9.5

18. 101 114 128 106 125 122 120 114 116

19. 4.25 4.46 4.19 4.23 4.25 4.28 4.27 4.35

20. 11 15 18 22 25 29 32 36 39 41 42 45 48 51

Make a box-and-whisker plot for each set of values.

21. 2 8 3 7 3 6 4 9 10 15 21 29 32 30 5 7 32 4 11 13 11 14 10 12 13 15

22. 1054 1165 1287 1385 1456 1398 1298 1109 1067 1384 1499 1032 1222 1045

23. 43.4 46.5 47.9 51.0 50.2 49.5 42.5 41.6 46.8 50.0

24. 19 20 21 22 23 25 27 12 19 31 53 52 48 41 29 33 48 46 44 42

Find the values at the 20th and 80th percentiles for each set of values.

25. 188 168 174 198 186 178 184 190 176 172 170 180 182 186 176

26. 376 324 346 348 350 352 356 368 345 360

27. 98 99 96 94 95 96 97 99 95 94 93 96 97 98 99 97 96 94 92 97

28. 2 12 17 20 22 28 32 37 38 41 44 51 53 59 62 78 86 92 102 112

29. The data shows the average temperatures in January for several cities in the mid-South.
49.1 50.8 42.9 44.0 44.2 51.4 45.7 39.9 50.8 46.7 52.4 50.4

   a. Find the mean of the temperatures.

   b. Find the median of the temperatures.

   c. Find the mode of the temperatures.

   d. Find the quartiles of the data. Sketch a box-and-whisker plot, and label the quartiles.

Practice 12-4

Find the mean and the standard deviation for each set of values. Round to the nearest tenth.

1. 232 254 264 274 287 298 312 342 398

2. 26 27 28 28 28 29 30 30 32 35 35 36

3. 2.2 2.2 2.3 2.4 2.4 2.4 2.5 2.5 2.5 2.6

4. 75 73 77 79 79 74 81 74 70 68 70 72

5. 87 21 90 43 54 23 123 110 90 44 50

Find the range, mean, and interquartile range of each set of values.

6. 10 12 13 10 9 5 6 11   **7.** 23 56 59 60 123 164 180 212

8. 524 526 532 531 534 539 530 535   **9.** 1.4 1.6 1.9 2.2 2.6 2.7 2.9 3.1

10. 45 48 46 47 45 48 46 49 46 47   **11.** 97 102 99 105 100 101 99 101

Determine the number of standard deviations that includes all data values.

12. The mean test score on a standardized test is 216; the standard deviation is 52.
127 98 236 192 267 335 217 365 472 177

13. The mean age of students in a school is 16.4 years; the standard deviation is 1.5.
13 17 18 15 16 14 15 18 17 16 15 16 13

14. The average rainfall for the month of April for several Eastern cities is as follows:
3.0 3.4 4.3 3.6 3.6 2.9 2.8 3.9 2.8 2.9 4.5 3.8 4.2 3.6 4.0 2.9 3.1
   a. Find the mean of the data.
   b. Find the standard deviation of the data.
   c. Find the range of the data.
   d. Within how many standard deviations is a rainfall of 2.8 in.? 4.0 in.?

15. The test scores on a college algebra test are as follows:
67 69 71 75 78 78 83 85 85 85 85 86 87 89 92 95 98 98 98 100
100 100 100 100 100 100
   a. Find the range of the data.
   b. Find the interquartile range.
   c. Find the mean of the data.
   d. Find the standard deviation.
   e. Within how many standard deviations of the mean is a score of 65?
   f. Within how many standard deviations of the mean is a score of 100?

16. A set of values has a mean of 67 and a standard deviation of 8. Find the z-score of the value 70.

17. A set of values has a mean of 102 and a standard deviation of 12. Find the z-score of the value 135.

Practice 12-5

1. In a survey, participants were asked their opinion of a new government program. The response scale ranged from 1 to 4, with 4 being a favorable response to the program. Which sample was largest? Explain.

Sample	Score	Standard Deviation
A	3.0	1.1
B	2.8	1.3
C	2.9	0.8

Identify any bias in each sampling method. When appropriate, suggest a sampling method that is more likely to produce a random sample.

2. A committee wants to find how much time students spend reading each week. They ask the students as they enter the library.

3. The students planning the junior class party want to know what kinds of pizza to buy. They ask the pizza restaurant what kinds sell the most.

4. The county road department wants to know which roads cause the most concern among the residents of the county. They ask the local restaurant to hand out survey forms.

5. A politician wants to know what issues are most important to the voters in his district. He spends all day Tuesday talking to people as they enter the grocery store.

6 A politician wants to know the voters' views on an important issue. She has her campaign workers call people randomly from the phone book.

Find the sample size that produces each margin of error.

7. ±15%   **8.** ±2%   **9.** ±0.9%   **10.** ±0.6%

For each sample find the sample proportion, the margin of error, and an interval likely to contain the true population proportion. Round to the nearest percent.

11. In a survey of 38 parents of preschool children, 20 would like to have their local school district provide play group sessions at least one evening a month.

12. In a random sample of 526 visitors to the craft center, 378 want the craft center to be open later in the evenings.

13. In a survey of 165 visitors to the library, 102 want the library to have more novels available.

14. In one lake, 98 of the last 323 fish caught have a certain chemical present in their body.

15. In a traffic survey, 537 of the 1287 drivers passing through the checkpoint were traveling more than 100 miles from home.

Practice 12-6

1. The probability that a baby is a male is 50%. Use a tree diagram to find each probability.

   a. P(at least 1 baby in a family with 3 children is a male)

   b. P(at least 2 babies in a family of 3 children are male)

   c. P(exactly 2 of 3 babies born in the hospital on any day are male)

For each situation, describe a trial and a success. Then design and run a simulation to find the probability.

2. The probability that the weather will be acceptable for a launch of the space shuttle over the next 3 days is 70% each day. Find the probability that the weather will be acceptable at least one of the next three days.

3. A poll shows that 30% of the voters favor an earlier curfew. Find the probability that all of five people chosen at random favor an earlier curfew.

4. The probability that a machine part is defective is 10%. Find the probability that exactly one part is defective in a sample of five parts.

Find the probability of x successes in n trials for the given probability of success p on each trial.

5. $x = 5, n = 5, p = 0.4$

6. $x = 2, n = 8, p = 0.9$

7. $x = 3, n = 10, p = 0.25$

8. $x = 1, n = 3, p = 0.2$

Use the binomial expansion of $(p + q)^n$ to calculate and graph each binomial distribution.

9. $n = 5, p = 0.6$

10. $n = 3, p = 0.7$

11. $n = 3, p = 0.1$

12. $n = 4, p = 0.8$

13. There is a 60% probability of rain each of the next 5 days. Find each probability. Round to the nearest percent.

   a. P(rain at least 3 of the next 5 days)

   b. P(rain at least 1 of the next 5 days)

   c. P(rain at least 1 of the next 4 days)

   d. P(rain at least 1 of the next 2 days)

14. In one area the probability of a power outage during a rainstorm is 4%. Find each probability. Round to the nearest percent.

   a. P(at least 1 outage in the next 5 rainstorms)

   b. P(at least 2 outages in the next 10 rainstorms)

   c. P(at least 1 outage in the next 20 rainstorms)

Practice 12-7

A set of data with a mean of 45 and a standard deviation of 8.3 is normally distributed. Find each value, given its distance from the mean.

1. +1 standard deviation from the mean

2. +3 standard deviations from the mean

3. −1 standard deviation from the mean

4. −2 standard deviations from the mean

Sketch a normal curve for each distribution. Label the *x*-axis at one, two, and three standard deviations from the mean.

5. mean = 95; standard deviation = 12

6. mean = 100; standard deviation = 15

7. mean = 60; standard deviation = 6

8. mean = 23.8; standard deviation = 5.2

9. mean = 676; standard deviation = 60

10. mean = 54.2; standard deviation = 12.3

A set of data has a normal distribution with a mean of 5.1 and a standard deviation of 0.9. Find the percent of data within each interval.

11. between 4.2 and 5.1

12. between 6.0 and 6.9

13. greater than 6.9

14. between 4.2 and 6.0

15. less than 4.2

16. less than 5.1

17. Scores on an exam are normally distributed with a mean of 76 and a standard deviation of 10.

   a. In a group of 230 tests, how many students score above 96?

   b. In a group of 230 tests, how many students score below 66?

   c. In a group of 230 tests, how many students score within one standard deviation of the mean?

18. The number of nails of a given length is normally distributed with a mean length of 5.00 in. and a standard deviation of 0.03 in.

   a. Find the number of nails in a bag of 120 that are less than 4.94 in. long.

   b. Find the number of nails in a bag of 120 that are between 4.97 and 5.03 in. long.

   c. Find the number of nails in a bag of 120 that are over 5.03 in. long.

19. The actual weights of bags of pet food are normally distributed. The mean of the weights is 50.0 lb, with a standard deviation of 0.2 lb. Use the graph for a–c.

   a. About what percent of bags of pet food weigh less than 49.8 lb?

   b. In a group of 250 bags, how many would you expect to weigh more than 50.4 lb?

   c. In a group of 50 bags, how many would you expect to be within 1.5 standard deviations of the mean?

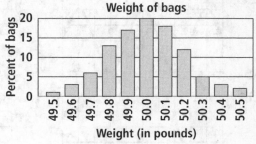

Weight of bags

Percent of bags

Weight (in pounds)

Practice 13-1

Determine whether each function *is* or *is not* periodic. If it is, find
the period.

1.
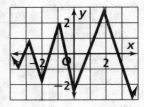

2.
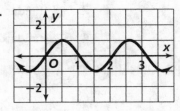

3.
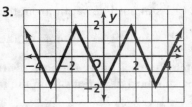

For each function, identify one cycle in two different ways. Then determine
the period of the function.

4.
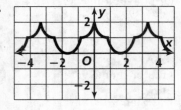

5.
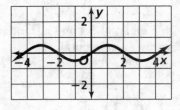

6.
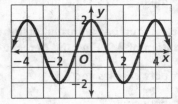

Find the period and amplitude of each periodic function.

7.
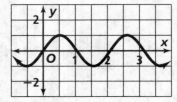

8.
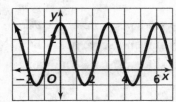

9.
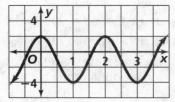

10.
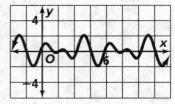

11.
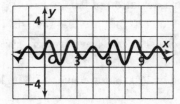

12.
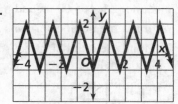

13.
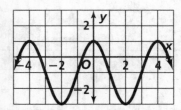

14.
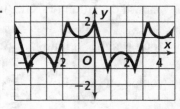

15.
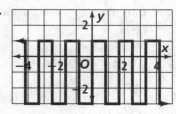

16.
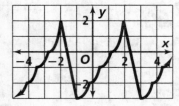

17.
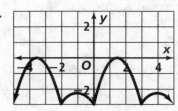

18.
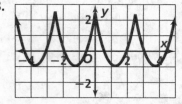

Practice 13-2

Angles and the Unit Circle

Sketch each angle in standard position.

1. 30° **2.** 60° **3.** 100° **4.** 135° **5.** 210°

6. 270° **7.** 330° **8.** −30° **9.** −90° **10.** −190°

11. −150° **12.** −330° **13.** −45° **14.** 315° **15.** −180°

16. 120° **17.** −120° **18.** 145° **19.** −145° **20.** −355°

Find the measure of an angle between 0° and 360° coterminal with each given angle.

21. −100° **22.** −60° **23.** −225° **24.** −145° **25.** 372°

26. −15° **27.** 482° **28.** 484° **29.** −20° **30.** 421°

31. 409° **32.** −38° **33.** 376° **34.** −210° **35.** 387°

36. 390° **37.** 660° **38.** 440° **39.** −170° **40.** 370°

41. −700° **42.** 458° **43.** 480° **44.** 406° **45.** −120°

46. 460° **47.** −222° **48.** −330° **49.** −127° **50.** 377°

Find the exact coordinates of the point where the terminal side of the given angle intersects the unit circle. Then find the decimal equivalents. Round your answers to the nearest hundredth.

51. 45° **52.** 225° **53.** −225° **54.** −45° **55.** 330°

56. −330° **57.** 150° **58.** −150° **59.** 300° **60.** −300°

61. 240° **62.** 120° **63.** −90° **64.** 360° **65.** 720°

66.

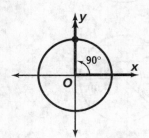

67.

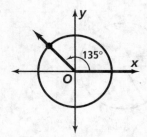

68.

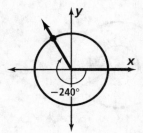

Find the measure of each angle in standard position.

69.

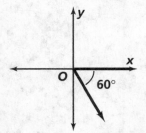

70.

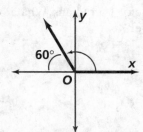

71.

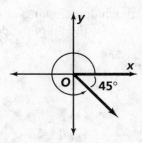

Practice 13-3

Radian Measure

Write each measure in radians. Express your answer in terms of **π**.

1. 45° **2.** 90° **3.** 30° **4.** 150° **5.** 180°

6. 240° **7.** 270° **8.** 300° **9.** 360° **10.** 40°

11. 80° **12.** 110° **13.** 160° **14.** 200° **15.** 220°

Write each measure in degrees. Round your answer to the nearest
degree, if necessary.

16. π **17.** 2π **18.** $\frac{5\pi}{6}$ **19.** $\frac{3\pi}{4}$ **20.** $\frac{3\pi}{2}$

21. $\frac{\pi}{6}$ **22.** $\frac{7\pi}{6}$ **23.** $\frac{11\pi}{6}$ **24.** $\frac{\pi}{3}$ **25.** $\frac{4\pi}{3}$

26. $\frac{5\pi}{4}$ **27.** $\frac{7\pi}{4}$ **28.** $\frac{2\pi}{3}$ **29.** $\frac{\pi}{9}$ **30.** $\frac{2\pi}{9}$

The measure *θ* of an angle in standard position is given. Find the exact
values of cos *θ* and sin *θ* for each angle measure.

31. $\frac{\pi}{6}$ radians **32.** $\frac{\pi}{3}$ radians **33.** $-\frac{3\pi}{4}$ radians **34.** $\frac{7\pi}{4}$ radians

35. $\frac{5\pi}{6}$ radians **36.** $\frac{4\pi}{3}$ radians **37.** $\frac{11\pi}{6}$ radians **38.** $\frac{2\pi}{3}$ radians

Use each circle to find the length of the indicated arc. Round your answer to
the nearest tenth.

39.
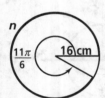

40.
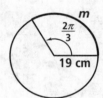

41.
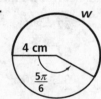

42.
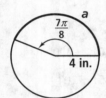

43.
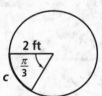

44.
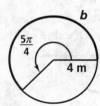

45. A pendulum swings through an angle of 1.8 radians. The distance the
tip of the pendulum travels is 32 in. How long is the pendulum?

46. A 0.8 m pendulum swings through an angle of 1.5 radians. What
distance does the tip of the pendulum travel?

Practice 13-4

The Sine Function

Find the amplitude and period of each sine curve. Then write an equation for each curve.

1.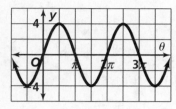

2.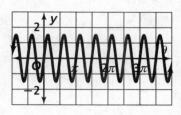

3.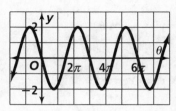

4.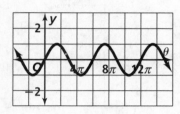

5.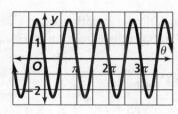

6.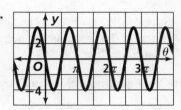

Sketch one cycle of each sine curve. Assume $a > 0$. Write an equation for each graph.

7. amplitude = 2; period = π

8. amplitude = 3; period = 2π

9. amplitude = 2; period = $\frac{\pi}{2}$

10. amplitude = 2; period = $\frac{\pi}{4}$

11. amplitude = 1.5; period = $\frac{\pi}{3}$

12. amplitude = 2.5; period = 2π

Sketch one cycle of the graph of each sine function.

13. $y = 2 \sin \theta$

14. $y = -2 \sin 4\theta$

15. $y = \sin 2\theta$

16. $y = 3 \sin \frac{\theta}{2}$

17. $y = -\sin 2\theta$

18. $y = -5 \sin 3\theta$

19. $y = -3 \sin 2\theta$

20. $y = 4 \sin 5\theta$

21. $y = -4 \sin \frac{\theta}{2}$

Use the graph at the right to find the value of $y = 0.3 \sin \theta$ for each value of θ.

22. 6 radians

23. $\frac{\pi}{4}$ radians

24. $\frac{3\pi}{4}$ radians

25. $\frac{\pi}{2}$ radian

Use the graph at the right to find the value of $y = 0.3 \sin \theta$ for each value of θ.

26. 160°

27. 135°

28. 270°

29. 225°

Practice 13-5

The Cosine Function

Sketch the graph of each function in the interval from 0 to 2π.

1. $y = \cos \theta$

2. $y = 2 \cos \pi\theta$

3. $y = 5 \cos \theta$

4. $y = -\cos \theta$

5. $y = -5 \cos \theta$

6. $y = \cos 2\pi\theta$

7. $y = -2 \cos 2\theta$

8. $y = 3 \cos 4\theta$

9. $y = \cos \frac{\theta}{2}$

10. $y = 3 \cos 8\theta$

11. $y = -4 \cos \pi\theta$

12. $y = 0.5 \cos \pi\theta$

13. $y = -\cos 2\theta$

14. $y = -3 \cos \frac{\pi}{2}\theta$

15. $y = 4 \cos \pi\theta$

16. Suppose 12 in. waves occur every 5 s. Write an equation using a cosine function that models the height of a water particle as it moves from crest to crest.

Write the equation of a cosine function for each graph.

17.
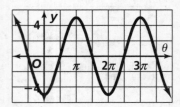

18.
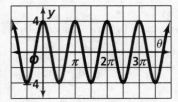

19.
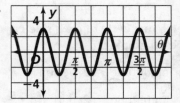

Find the period and amplitude of each cosine function. Identify where the maximum value, minimum value, and zeros occur in the interval from 0 to 2π.

20.
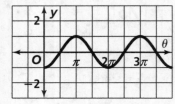

21.
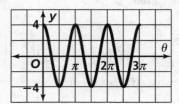

22.
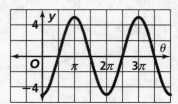

Solve each equation in the interval from 0 to 2π. Round to the nearest hundredth.

23. $2 \cos 3\theta = 1.5$

24. $\cot \frac{t}{3} = 1$

25. $1.5 \cos \pi\theta = -1.5$

26. $3 \cos \frac{\pi}{5}\theta = 2$

27. $3 \cos t = 2$

28. $0.5 \cos \frac{\theta}{2} = 0.5$

29. $4 \cos \frac{\pi}{4}\theta = -2$

30. $3 \cos \frac{\theta}{4} = 1.5$

31. $3 \cos \theta = -3$

Write a cosine function for each description. Assume that $a > 0$.

32. amplitude $= 2\pi$, period $= 1$

33. amplitude $= \frac{1}{2}$, period $= \pi$

Practice 13-6

Identify the period and tell where the asymptotes occur, in the interval from 0 to 2π, for each function.

1. $y = \tan \theta$

2. $y = 2 \tan \frac{\theta}{2}$

3. $y = 3 \tan \frac{\theta}{4}$

4. $y = 4 \tan 2\theta$

5. $y = -\tan \frac{\pi}{2}\theta$

6. $y = -2 \tan \pi\theta$

7. $y = -3 \tan 2\theta$

8. $y = -4 \tan \theta$

9. $y = 0.5 \tan \pi\theta$

Sketch two cycles of the graph of each function.

10. $y = \tan \theta$

11. $y = 2 \tan \theta$

12. $y = -\tan \theta$

13. $y = -2 \tan \theta$

14. $y = -0.5 \tan 2\theta$

15. $y = 3 \tan \theta$

16. $y = -3 \tan 2\theta$

17. $y = 5 \tan \frac{\pi}{2}\theta$

18. $y = 2 \tan 3\theta$

19. $y = 0.5 \tan 2\theta$

20. $y = -2.5 \tan \frac{\pi}{2}\theta$

21. $y = -5 \tan 2\pi\theta$

22. $y = -2 \tan 4\theta$

23. $y = -0.25 \tan 3\theta$

24. $y = -4 \tan 4\pi\theta$

25. $y = -2.25 \tan \theta$

26. $y = -0.25 \tan \frac{\pi}{3}\theta$

27. $y = 0.75 \tan 4\theta$

Identify the period of each tangent function.

28.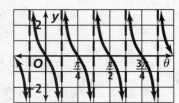

29.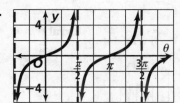

30.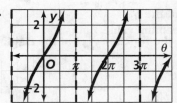

Use the graph of $y = \tan \theta$ to find each value. If the tangent is undefined at that point, write *undefined*.

31. $\tan \frac{\pi}{2}$

32. $\tan \left(-\frac{3\pi}{4}\right)$

33. $\tan \left(-\frac{\pi}{4}\right)$

34. $\tan \frac{3\pi}{2}$

Using your graphing calculator, graph each function on the interval $0° < x < 470°$ and $-300 < y < 300$. Evaluate the function at $x = 45°, 90°,$ and $135°$.

35. $y = 200 \tan x$

36. $y = -75 \tan \left(\frac{1}{4}x\right)$

37. $y = -50 \tan x$

Practice 13-7

Graph each function in the interval from 0 to 2π.

1. $y = -\sin\left(x + \frac{\pi}{2}\right)$ **2.** $y = 3\sin\left(x - \frac{\pi}{4}\right) + 2$ **3.** $y = \cos\frac{1}{2}x + 1$

4. $y = 3\cos(x - 2)$ **5.** $y = \sin 3(x - \pi)$ **6.** $y = \cos(x + 4)$

7. $y = \cos x + 3$ **8.** $y = -2\sin x + 1$ **9.** $y = -\cos 2\left(x + \frac{\pi}{4}\right)$

10. $y = \frac{1}{2}\cos x + 3$ **11.** $y = \sin\frac{1}{2}(x + \pi)$ **12.** $y = \cos\left(x + \frac{\pi}{6}\right)$

13. $y = -2\cos x + 3$ **14.** $y = \sin 2x + 1$ **15.** $y = \sin 2\left(x - \frac{\pi}{3}\right)$

Write an equation for each translation.

16. $y = \sin x$, 2 units down   **17.** $y = \cos x$, π units left

18. $y = \cos x$, $\frac{\pi}{4}$ units up   **19.** $y = \sin x$, 3.2 units to the right

Find the amplitude and period of each function. Describe any phase shift and vertical shift in the graph.

20. $y = 3\cos x + 2$ **21.** $y = -2\sin\left(x + \frac{\pi}{2}\right)$ **22.** $y = \cos 2x + 1$

23. $y = -\sin\left(x - \frac{\pi}{3}\right)$ **24.** $y = \frac{1}{2}\cos x - 3$ **25.** $y = \cos\frac{1}{2}x - 2$

Use the function $f(x)$ at the right. Graph each translation.

26. $f(x) + 3$ **27.** $f(x + 1)$

28. $f(x) - 5$ **29.** $f(x + 3)$

30. $f(x + 2) - 1$ **31.** $f(x) - 4$

What is the value of h in each translation? Describe each phase shift (use a phrase like *3 units to the left*).

32. $g(x) = f(x + 2)$ **33.** $g(x) = f(x - 1)$ **34.** $h(t) = f(t + 1.5)$

35. $f(x) = g(x - 1)$ **36.** $y = \cos\left(x - \frac{\pi}{2}\right)$ **37.** $y = \cos(x + \pi)$

Practice 13-8

Reciprocal Trigonometric Functions

Evaluate each expression. Each angle is given in radians. Round to the nearest thousandth, if necessary.

1. $\cot 4$

2. $\csc \frac{\pi}{6}$

3. $\csc (-2)$

4. $\sec \pi$

5. $\cot (-\pi)$

6. $\sec (-3.5)$

7. $\cot \frac{\pi}{3}$

8. $\sec 1.5$

9. $\csc (-1.5)$

10. $\cot \pi$

11. $\sec 3$

12. $\csc \frac{\pi}{4}$

Evaluate each expression. Write your answer in exact form. If appropriate, also state it as a decimal rounded to the nearest hundredth. If the expression is undefined, write *undefined*.

13. $\sec 45°$

14. $\cot 180°$

15. $\sec 30°$

16. $\csc 30°$

17. $\cot (-180°)$

18. $\csc (-45°)$

19. $\csc 180°$

20. $\cot 45°$

21. $\sec 90°$

22. $\sec (-30°)$

23. $\csc (-60°)$

24. $\sec 60°$

25. Suppose $\tan \theta = \frac{6}{9}$. Find $\cot \theta$

26. Suppose $\sin \theta = \frac{2}{5}$. Find $\csc \theta$

27. Suppose $\cos \theta = \frac{14}{20}$. Find $\sec \theta$

28. Suppose $\tan \theta = -\frac{2}{3}$. Find $\cot \theta$

Graph each function in the interval from 0 to 2π.

29. $y = \cot 2\theta$

30. $y = -\cot \frac{1}{2}\theta$

31. $y = \sec \left(\theta - \frac{\pi}{2}\right)$

32. $y = \csc 2\theta + 1$

33. $y = -\csc 3\theta$

34. $y = \sec \theta + 2$

35. $y = \cot (\theta + \pi)$

36. $y = \sec \frac{1}{4}\theta$

37. $y = \csc \theta - 1$

Use the graph of the appropriate reciprocal trigonometric function to find each value. Round to the nearest thousandth, if necessary.

38. $\cot 30°$

39. $\csc 180°$

40. $\cot 70°$

41. $\sec 100°$

42. $\sec 50°$

43. $\csc 100°$

44. $\cot 20°$

45. $\sec 120°$

46. A fire truck is parked on the shoulder of a freeway next to a long wall. The red light on the top of the truck rotates through one complete revolution every 2 seconds. The function $y = 10 \sec \pi t$ models the length of the beam in feet to a point on the wall in terms of time t.

   a. Graph the function.

   b. Find the length at time 1.75 seconds

   c. Find the length at time 2 seconds.

Practice 14-1

Verify each identity.

1. $\sin \theta \sec \theta \cot \theta = 1$

2. $\csc \theta = \cot \theta \sec \theta$

3. $\dfrac{\sin \theta}{\csc \theta} = \sin^2 \theta$

4. $\cos \theta \csc \theta \tan \theta = 1$

5. $\sin \theta \tan \theta + \cos \theta = \sec \theta$

6. $\dfrac{\csc \theta}{\cot \theta} = \sec \theta$

7. $\sec \theta = \tan \theta \csc \theta$

8. $\tan \theta + \cot \theta = \sec \theta \csc \theta$

9. $\tan^2 \theta + 1 = \sec^2 \theta$

10. $\cos \theta \cot \theta + \sin \theta = \csc \theta$

11. $\dfrac{\sec \theta}{\csc \theta} = \tan \theta$

12. $\sec \theta \cot \theta = \csc \theta$

13. $\sec^2 \theta - \tan^2 \theta = 1$

14. $\sec \theta = \csc \theta \tan \theta$

15. $\dfrac{\sin \theta + \cos \theta}{\sin \theta} = 1 + \cot \theta$

16. $\cos \theta (\sec \theta - \cos \theta) = \sin^2 \theta$

17. $\cot \theta \sec \theta = \csc \theta$

18. $(1 - \sin \theta)(1 + \sin \theta) = \cos^2 \theta$

Simplify each trigonometric expression.

19. $1 - \sec^2 \theta$

20. $\dfrac{\sec \theta}{\tan \theta}$

21. $\csc \theta \tan \theta$

22. $\sec \theta \cos^2 \theta$

23. $\csc^2 \theta - \cot^2 \theta$

24. $1 - \sin^2 \theta$

25. $\tan \theta \cot \theta$

26. $\cos \theta \cot \theta + \sin \theta$

27. $\cos \theta \tan \theta$

28. $\dfrac{\sin \theta \cot \theta}{\cos \theta}$

29. $\sec \theta \tan \theta \csc \theta$

30. $\sec \theta \cot \theta$

31. $\dfrac{\sin \theta}{\csc \theta} + \dfrac{\cos \theta}{\sec \theta}$

32. $\dfrac{\tan \theta \csc \theta}{\sec \theta}$

33. $\cot^2 \theta - \csc^2 \theta$

34. $\dfrac{\cot \theta}{\csc \theta}$

Practice 14-2

Solving Trigonometric Equations Using Inverses

Solve each equation for $0 \le \theta < 2\pi$.

1. $2 \tan \theta + 2 = 0$

2. $2 \cos \theta = 1$

3. $2 \cos \theta + \sqrt{3} = 0$

4. $\sqrt{3} \cot \theta - 1 = 0$

5. $4 \sin \theta - 3 = 0$

6. $4 \sin \theta + 3 = 0$

7. $\left(2 \cos \theta + \sqrt{3}\right)(2 \cos \theta + 1) = 0$

8. $\sqrt{3} \tan \theta - 2 \sin \theta \tan \theta = 0$

9. $2 \cos^2 \theta + \cos \theta = 0$

10. $5 \cos \theta - 3 = 0$

11. $\tan \theta - 2 \cos \theta \tan \theta = 0$

12. $\tan \theta (\tan \theta + 1) = 0$

13. $(\cos \theta - 1)(2 \cos \theta - 1) = 0$

14. $\tan^2 \theta - \tan \theta = 0$

15. If a projectile is fired into the air with an initial velocity v at an angle of elevation θ, then the height h of the projectile at time t is given by $h = -16t^2 + vt \sin \theta$.

   a. Find the angle of elevation θ of a rifle barrel, to the nearest tenth of a degree, if a bullet fired at 1500 ft/s takes 2 s to reach a height of 750 ft.

   b. Find the angle of elevation of a rifle, to the nearest tenth of a degree, if a bullet fired at 1500 ft/s takes 3 s to reach a height of 750 ft.

Use a calculator and inverse functions to find the radian measures of the angles.

16. angles whose tangent is 2.5

17. angles whose sine is 0.75

18. angles whose cosine is (-0.24)

19. angles whose cosine is 0.45

Use a unit circle and 45°–45°–90° triangles to find the degree measures of the angles.

20. angles whose sine is $\dfrac{\sqrt{2}}{2}$

21. angles whose tangent is 1

22. angles whose cosine is $\dfrac{\sqrt{2}}{2}$

23. angle whose sine is 1

Use the graph of the inverse of $y = \cos \theta$ at the right.

24. Find the measures of the angles whose cosine is -1.

25. Find the measures of the angles whose cosine is 0.

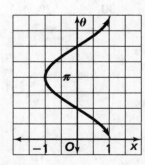

Practice 14-3

Right Triangles and Trigonometric Ratios

Use the triangle at the right to find the exact values of the
trigonometric ratios.

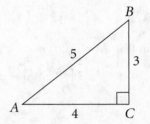

1. $\cos A$ **2.** $\cos B$

3. $\tan A$ **4.** $\tan B$

5. $\cot B$ **6.** $\sec A$

7. $\csc A$ **8.** $\sin B$

**In $\triangle DEF$, $\angle D$ is a right angle. Find the remaining sides and angles.
Round answers to the nearest tenth.**

9. $f = 8$, $e = 15$ **10.** $f = 1$, $d = 2$ **11.** $f = 1$, $e = 2$ **12.** $f = 2$, $e = 1$

13. $f = 1$, $d = 500$ **14.** $d = 21$, $e = 8$ **15.** $e = 6$, $d = 12$ **16.** $e = 5$, $f = 1$

17. Suppose you are standing on one bank of a river. A tree on the other
side of the river is known to be 150 ft tall. A line from the top of the
tree to the ground at your feet makes an angle of 11° with the ground.
How far from you is the base of the tree?

18. A kite string makes a 62° angle with the horizontal, and 300 ft of string
is let out. The string is held 6 ft off the ground. How high is the kite?

19. You are designing several access ramps. What angle would each ramp
make with the ground, to the nearest 0.1°?

  a. 20 ft long, rises 16 in.   **b.** 8 ft long, rises 8 in.   **c.** 12 ft long, rises 6 in.

  d. 30 ft long, rises 32 in.   **e.** 4 ft long, rises 6 in.   **f.** 6 ft long, rises 14 in.

20. In $\triangle ABC$, $\angle C$ is a right angle and $\tan A = \frac{2}{3}$. Draw a diagram and find
each value in fraction form and in decimal form.

  a. $\cos A$ **b.** $\tan B$ **c.** $\sin A$

  d. $\cot B$ **e.** $\sec A$ **f.** $\csc B$

Find the measure of each angle to the nearest tenth of a degree.

21. $\sin^{-1}\left(\frac{\sqrt{2}}{2}\right)$ **22.** $\cos^{-1}(0.5)$ **23.** $\tan^{-1}\left(\sqrt{3}\right)$ **24.** $\sin^{-1}(0.3232)$

25. $\cos^{-1}(0.8)$ **26.** $\tan^{-1}(1)$ **27.** $\cos^{-1}(0.4)$ **28.** $\tan^{-1}(3.2678)$

29. $\sin^{-1}(0.75)$ **30.** $\tan^{-1}(0.5)$ **31.** $\tan^{-1}(12.0001)$ **32.** $\sin^{-1}(0.1044)$

Practice 14-4

Area and the Law of Sines

Use the Law of Sines. Find the measure of the indicated part of each triangle. Round answers to the nearest tenth.

1. Find $m\angle X$ if $x = 10$, $y = 12$, and $m\angle Y = 18°$.

2. Find x if $y = 21$, $m\angle X = 31°$, and $m\angle Y = 43°$.

3. Find z if $y = 15$, $m\angle Y = 79°$, and $m\angle Z = 79°$.

4. Find $m\angle Z$ if $y = 23$, $z = 19$, and $m\angle Y = 123°$.

5. Find y if $z = 54$, $m\angle Y = 65°$, and $m\angle Z = 21°$.

6. Find $m\angle Y$ if $y = 36$, $z = 42$, and $m\angle Z = 39°$.

7. Find $m\angle X$ if $x = 54$, $z = 63$, and $m\angle Z = 33°$.

8. Find x if $z = 18$, $m\angle X = 25°$, and $m\angle Z = 31°$.

9. Find x if $y = 20$, $m\angle X = 30°$, and $m\angle Y = 60°$.

10. Find $m\angle X$ if $x = 63$, $y = 72$, and $m\angle Y = 45°$.

11. Find $m\angle Z$ if $y = 7$, $z = 3$, and $m\angle Y = 31°$.

12. Find x if $y = 35$, $m\angle X = 118°$, and $m\angle Y = 20°$.

13. Find $m\angle X$ if $x = 9$, $y = 15$, and $m\angle Y = 62°$.

14. Find y if $z = 70$, $m\angle Y = 25°$, and $m\angle Z = 100°$.

Find the area of each triangle.

15.

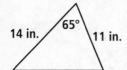

14 in.   65°   11 in.

16.

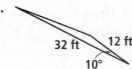

32 ft   12 ft   10°

17.

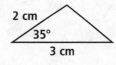

2 cm   35°   3 cm

18. A triangle has sides of lengths 15 in. and 22 in., and the measure of the angle between them is 95°. Find the area of the triangle.

19. A hot-air balloon is observed from two points, A and B, on the ground 800 ft apart as shown in the diagram. The angle of elevation of the balloon is 65° from point A and 37° from point B. Find the distance from point A to the balloon.

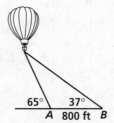

65°   37°
A 800 ft B

20. Two searchlights on the shore of a lake are located 3020 yd apart as shown in the diagram. A ship in distress is spotted from each searchlight. The beam from the first searchlight makes an angle of 38° with the baseline. The beam from the second light makes an angle of 57° with the baseline. Find the ship's distance from each searchlight.

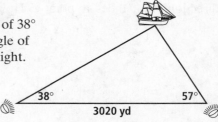

38°   57°
3020 yd

Practice 14-5

Use the Law of Cosines. Find the measure of the indicated part of each triangle. Round answers to the nearest tenth.

1. Find x if $y = 4$, $z = 9$, and $m\angle X = 16°$.

2. Find y if $x = 8$, $z = 5$, and $m\angle Y = 8°$.

3. Find $m\angle Y$ if $x = 17.2$, $y = 22.1$, and $z = 31.3$.

4. Find z if $x = 32$, $y = 25$, and $m\angle Z = 21°$.

5. Find $m\angle Y$ if $x = 14$, $y = 6$, and $z = 10$.

6. Find $m\angle X$ if $x = 24.9$, $y = 32.0$, and $z = 42.3$.

7. Find x if $y = 16$, $z = 4$, and $m\angle X = 123°$.

8. Find $m\angle Z$ if $x = 6.2$, $y = 5.9$, and $z = 3.4$.

9. Find z if $x = 321$, $y = 543$, and $m\angle Z = 54°$.

10. Find $m\angle Z$ if $x = 235$, $y = 154$, and $z = 239$.

11. Find x if $y = 10$, $z = 12$, and $m\angle X = 29°$.

12. Find y if $x = 3$, $z = 6$, and $m\angle Y = 15°$.

13. Find x if $y = 8$, $z = 7$, and $m\angle X = 149°$.

14. Find z if $x = 7$, $y = 22$, and $m\angle Z = 12°$.

15. Find z if $x = 46$, $y = 67$, and $m\angle Z = 85°$.

16. Find $m\angle X$ if $x = 4$, $y = 7$, and $z = 10$.

17. Find $m\angle Y$ if $x = 32$, $y = 79$, and $z = 86$.

18. Find $m\angle Z$ if $x = 3$, $y = 2.9$, and $z = 4.6$.

19. Find $m\angle Y$ if $x = 34.7$, $y = 18.9$, and $z = 21.5$.

20. Find $m\angle Z$ if $x = 14$, $y = 16$, and $z = 18$.

21. The sides of a triangular lot are 158 ft, 173 ft, and 191 ft. Find the measure of the angle opposite the longest side to the nearest tenth of a degree.

22. A car travels 50 miles due west from point A. At point B, the car turns and travels at an angle of 35° north of due east. The car travels in this direction for 40 miles, to point C. How far is point C from point A?

Practice 14-6 ....

Find each exact value. Use a sum or difference identity.

1. $\sin 240°$ **2.** $\tan(-300°)$ **3.** $\sin(-105°)$

4. $\cos 15°$ **5.** $\sin 15°$ **6.** $\sin 135°$

7. $\cos 225°$ **8.** $\tan 225°$ **9.** $\tan 240°$

10. $\cos 390°$ **11.** $\sin(-300°)$ **12.** $\tan(-75°)$

Verify each identity.

13. $\cot\left(\theta - \frac{\pi}{2}\right) = -\tan\theta$ **14.** $\sin\left(\theta - \frac{\pi}{2}\right) = -\cos\theta$

15. $\cos\left(\theta - \frac{\pi}{2}\right) = \sin\theta$ **16.** $\sec\left(\theta - \frac{\pi}{2}\right) = \csc\theta$

Use the definitions of the trigonometric ratios for a right triangle to derive each cofunction identity.

17. A cofunction identity for $\tan(90° - A)$

18. A cofunction identity for $\cos(90° - A)$

Solve each trigonometric equation for $0 \leq \theta < 2\pi$.

19. $2\sin\left(\frac{\pi}{2} - \theta\right)\tan\theta = 1$ **20.** $\cos\left(\frac{\pi}{2} - \theta\right)\tan\theta - \sec(-\theta) = 1$

21. $\sin^2\theta + \cos^2\theta = \tan\theta$ **22.** $2\sin^2\theta = \sin(-\theta)$

23. $\sqrt{3}\cos\left(\frac{\pi}{2} - \theta\right) = \cos(-\theta)$ **24.** $\cot\left(\frac{\pi}{2} - \theta\right) = \sin\theta$

25. $\csc\left(\frac{\pi}{2} - \theta\right) = \tan\theta$ **26.** $2\cos\left(\frac{\pi}{2} - \theta\right) = \tan(-\theta)$

27. $\csc^2\theta - \cot^2\theta = 2\cos\theta$ **28.** $\sin\left(\theta - \frac{\pi}{2}\right)\cos\theta = 0$

Use mental math to find the value of each trigonometric expression.

29. $\sin 10° \cos 80° + \cos 10° \sin 80°$

30. $\cos 110° \cos 70° - \sin 110° \sin 70°$

31. $\sin 310° \cos 130° - \cos 310° \sin 130°$

32. $\cos 95° \cos 50° + \sin 95° \sin 50°$

Practice 14-7

Double-Angle and Half-Angle Identities

Given $\sin \theta = \frac{7}{25}$ and $90° < \theta < 180°$, find the exact value of each expression.

1. $\cos \frac{\theta}{2}$ **2.** $\sin \frac{\theta}{2}$ **3.** $\tan \frac{\theta}{2}$

4. $\sec \frac{\theta}{2}$ **5.** $\csc \frac{\theta}{2}$ **6.** $\cot \frac{\theta}{2}$

Given $\cos \theta = -\frac{8}{17}$ and $180° < \theta < 270°$, find the exact value of each expression.

7. $\sin \frac{\theta}{2}$ **8.** $\cos \frac{\theta}{2}$ **9.** $\cot \frac{\theta}{2}$

10. $\tan \frac{\theta}{2}$ **11.** $\csc \frac{\theta}{2}$ **12.** $\sec \frac{\theta}{2}$

Use an angle sum identity to verify each identity.

13. $\cos 2\theta = \cos^2 \theta - \sin^2 \theta$ **14.** $\cos 2\theta = 2 \cos^2 \theta - 1$

15. $\cos 2\theta = 1 - 2 \sin^2 \theta$ **16.** $\sin 2\theta = 2 \sin \theta \cos \theta$

Verify each identity.

17. $\cos^2 \theta = \dfrac{1 + \cos 2\theta}{2}$ **18.** $\cot \theta = \dfrac{\sin 2\theta}{1 - \cos 2\theta}$

19. $\tan \theta + \cot \theta = 2 \csc 2\theta$ **20.** $\dfrac{\cos 2\theta}{\sin \theta \cos \theta} = \cot \theta - \tan \theta$

Use a double-angle identity to find the exact value of each expression.

21. $\sin 120°$ **22.** $\tan 600°$ **23.** $\sin 660°$

24. $\cos 660°$ **25.** $\tan 90°$ **26.** $\cos 90°$

27. $\tan 660°$ **28.** $\sin 240°$ **29.** $\tan 120°$

Use a half-angle identity to find the exact value of each expression.

30. $\cos 15°$ **31.** $\cos 7.5°$ **32.** $\tan 7.5°$

33. $\sin 7.5°$ **34.** $\cos 45°$ **35.** $\tan 22.5°$

36. $\cos 22.5°$ **37.** $\sin 90°$ **38.** $\cos 90°$